KETO
MEDITERRANEAN
COOKBOOK

Keto-Friendly Heart-Healthy Recipes for Weight Loss
on a Low-Carb Diet

Jennifer Tate

TABLE OF CONTENTS

BREAKFASTS

SNACKS

MEAT & POULTRY

FISH & SEAFOOD

SOUPS & SAUCES

VEGETABLES

DESSERTS

BAKING

INTRODUCTION

The idea for this book grew as I heard more and more stories in search of the **ideal diet for weight loss** and the deep dissatisfaction with all the rigid, bland diets that cost way too much for the average person to sustain. I can't remember when I didn't love food and cooking. I've been a professional chef for more than 15 years, and my ultimate goal is to create recipes and meal plans that are not only healthier and promote **weight loss but are also enjoyable, engaging, and sustainable.**

If nothing else, the pandemic years have shown us that we all can cook and eat healthy meals and do it with family and friends. This cookbook is my way of sharing my belief in the **long-term benefits of the keto Mediterranean diet.** I wanted to design an option that would appeal to as many people as possible and help them lead a life filled with delicious, satiating meals that made them leaner and healthier.

Before I share all my favorite keto Mediterranean recipes with you, we'll spend some time understanding the ins and outs of the Mediterranean and keto diets individually and learn a bit more about the basic nutrition underlying each of these diets and how it affects your body.

I hope you use this book as a guide to **creating a new lifestyle and eating habits** that will open up new experiences for you. I hope you are inspired to begin a journey to a healthier, happier, heart-healthy life filled with nutritious, delicious, and satisfying food.

KETO MEDITERRANEAN BASICS

The keto Mediterranean diet combines aspects of the Mediterranean diet with those of the keto diet. The goal is to optimize the health benefits achieved from both, including **weight loss, brain and heart health, and lower blood sugar and cholesterol levels.**

The keto Mediterranean diet includes many healthy options like fish, yogurt, vegetables, and olives while restricting certain carbs to increase metabolic activity and use ketones for energy. This diet focuses on clean eating, and by combining the two diets, we gain significant advantages and reduce the downsides associated with them individually.

THE MEDITERRANEAN DIET

This diet reflects the food traditions of the countries along the Mediterranean coast, including Italy, France, Spain, and Greece. It is simply how the people of the Mediterranean region have eaten for centuries.

Like the countries it originates, the Mediterranean diet bursts with aromatic herbs, flavorful ingredients, and various colors. It is indeed a **balanced and nutritious blend of foods** that will keep you satisfied and healthy. There are no specific rules; unlike the keto diet, you don't have to focus on specific macronutrients.

The Mediterranean diet leans toward a more plant-based approach using fruits and vegetables as its main dishes. This diet encourages you to slow down and appreciate the flavors of your food in what we may call a mindful way.

You can eat fresh fruits and vegetables and whole grains like oats, brown rice, corn, and pasta on this diet. Legumes, beans, peas, nuts, and seeds are also encouraged. **Protein comes from tuna, crab, salmon, sardines, trout, chicken, turkey, duck, and eggs.** These protein sources tend to be leaner and higher in omega-3 fatty acids, which are great for heart health. **Yogurt, cheese, olive oil, and avocado oil provide calcium and healthy fats.**

THE KETOGENIC DIET

Also known as the keto diet, the ketogenic diet has become increasingly popular over the last decade. It is a **high-fat, moderate-protein, low-carb diet** that aids in weight loss, can improve overall health, and may reduce symptoms of epilepsy and diabetes. Essentially, the keto diet drastically reduces carbohydrate consumption while increasing fat intake.

There are four main categories of the keto diet. They include:

1. *A standard ketogenic diet (SKD):* This is the most used diet, particularly for those who want to lose weight rapidly. In this keto option, 70% of your food intake comes from fat, 20% from protein, and the remaining 10% from carbohydrates.

2. *A targeted ketogenic diet (TKD):* This option follows the SKD model; the only difference is increasing your carbohydrate intake during training sessions or intense workouts.

3. *A cyclical ketogenic diet (CKD):* As the name suggests, in this adaptation of the diet, you cycle through five days of the SKD, and on the other two days, you have a high-carbohydrate intake. This version was created as a way to help balance out your body's carbohydrate needs so as not to feel as many withdrawal effects.

4. *High-protein ketogenic diet:* You increase your protein intake in this diet version. So your daily food consumption would be 60% fat, 35% protein, and 5% carbohydrates.

On the keto diet, you are encouraged to eat steak, ham, sausage, bacon, chicken, red meat, and fish like trout, tuna, and salmon. You can also enjoy eggs, cream, butter, cheese, nuts, seeds, extra-virgin olive oil, and avocado oil. You can eat vegetables as long as they are low in carbohydrates, like tomatoes, onions, broccoli, green peppers, asparagus, and cucumbers. However, you must avoid or restrict your intake of grains, beans, legumes, and fruit because of their higher carbohydrate content. You should also avoid sugary foods and foods that are processed.

The ketogenic diet triggers your body to use fat as its primary source of fuel for energy instead of glucose. Usually, when you consume large amounts of carbohydrates, your body breaks them down into simple sugars or glucose, which is stored as energy. Any excess is stored as fat. If you start eating fewer carbohydrates, your body will quickly run out of its regular energy source and have to switch to using the stored fat in your body. This usually takes about three to four days.

When this occurs, your body moves into ketosis. The liver breaks down the fat in your body. This action produces ketones (basically a by-product of your metabolism) used for energy since there is no glucose. If this process is sustained, it leads to increased weight loss.

Because of its higher fat content, the keto diet tends to be more filling which means there is reduced stimulation of hunger hormones. As a result, you eat fewer calories and lose more weight. However, the lack of dietary fiber in this diet can lead to indigestion and constipation. The keto diet can result in nutrient deficiencies if done over an extended period. Some people even experience the "keto flu," which includes headaches, irritability, fatigue, and weakness. These symptoms usually dissipate after the first week as your body moves into a state of ketosis. The keto diet is usually a short-term solution for rapid weight loss.

THE KETOGENIC MEDITERRANEAN DIET

So far, we've looked at the keto and Mediterranean diets individually to understand how they work and their benefits and downsides. Now, we'll combine the best of these two diets to create an incredible hybrid that can lead to a longer, healthier life.

This diet utilizes the carbohydrate restriction and fat inclusion of the keto diet with the whole foods and holistic lifestyle of the Mediterranean diet to create a **nutritious, sustainable way of eating and living.**

Basically, you will be consuming a Mediterranean diet, but you will be adjusting your carbohydrate intake to suit the keto diet to remain in that state of ketosis. Your protein will primarily come from seafood, poultry, and eggs, while you'll opt for keto-friendly vegetables that are low in carbohydrates. Remember, too, that the Mediterranean diet is holistic and includes physical activity. This remains an essential component of the keto Mediterranean diet.

HOW DOES IT WORK?

We've got a snapshot of how the Mediterranean and keto diets work individually, and we can understand how combining the best parts of each of these diets can create an almost **perfect diet that is easy to follow and not heavily restrictive.** The keto diet focuses on the macronutrients, while the Mediterranean diet ensures that the body receives the essential micronutrients.

The keto Mediterranean diet offers you the variety, flavor, and color of the Mediterranean diet while lowering your carbohydrate intake to help you lose weight and maintain that weight loss.

All the ingredients and foods found in this diet are readily available. Unlike the traditional keto diet, there isn't a strict emphasis on counting your macronutrients. This makes it easier to stick with the diet for the long term. Unlike the keto diet, this hybrid is more inclusive, allowing for vegetarian and vegan plans.

Additionally, this combination has incredible health benefits. The keto Mediterranean diet may help **control blood sugar and cholesterol levels, improve heart health, and lower your risk of inflammation.** Not to mention, it promotes weight loss and improves the body's insulin sensitivity.

Overall, the keto Mediterranean diet is a great choice for most who are looking for a healthier option that is feasible and flexible enough to work with their lifestyle. Let's take a closer look at how this combination works so well in terms of the macronutrients and the micronutrients needed by the body.

MACRONUTRIENTS

The macronutrients are those compounds that give us energy when consumed. The macronutrients are broken down into carbohydrates, fats, and protein. Most foods contain some combination of these three, but we generally classify the food based on which macronutrients it has more. As we've already learned, the traditional keto diet focuses on the combination of these macronutrients.

CARBOHYDRATES

Carbohydrates are normally what the body converts to glucose to use as fuel for energy. They are the only macronutrient that triggers the release of the hormone serotonin, which is linked to pleasure and happiness. This is sometimes why we overeat foods high in carbohydrates. In its simplest form, carbohydrates are glucose and fructose. If the body has more carbohydrates than it can use, the excess is stored as fat, leading to weight gain and health problems.

FATS

Fat is an intrinsic part of your body's structures and organs. In fact, about 60% of your brain is made up of fat. Your body also needs fatty acids to produce hormones critical for our body's functioning. Moreover, we need fat to absorb fat-soluble vitamins A, D, E, and K. It is also a significant energy source. Basically, fat is an essential macronutrient, and your body cannot produce all the fat it needs.

Fats are grouped into saturated and unsaturated fats. Saturated fats can remain solid at room temperature and are usually derived from animal sources. It is not recommended that you consume high amounts of saturated fats, but if you are following any version of the keto diet, then your body has adjusted to burning fat as fuel, so you should not have any problems.

Unsaturated fats can be monounsaturated and polyunsaturated. Monounsaturated fats are liquid at room temperature and come from nuts, seeds, olives, and avocados. The Mediterranean diet, as well as the keto diet opt for foods that have monounsaturated fats. Polyunsaturated fats include those high in omega-3 and omega-6 fatty acids. Omega-6 fatty acids are easily found in most diets in vegetable oils. They can increase or reduce inflammation in the body depending on the amount consumed. Omega-3 fatty acids benefit our health, but we tend to get less of them. It is found in fish, algae, walnuts, flaxseeds, and chia seeds.

PROTEIN

Our bodies use protein to build and maintain muscle and tissue. Almost every part of your body requires protein for its proper functioning. All proteins are composed of amino acids. There are nine basic amino acids that our bodies need but that we are unable to make. We have to get them through food. You can get protein from animal and plant sources. These include chicken, fish, eggs, milk, yogurt, nuts, and seeds. Beans and legumes are great sources of protein. Still, for the keto Mediterranean diet, they are too high in carbohydrates to be used. For this diet, protein intake should be about two grams for every kilogram of body weight.

MICRONUTRIENTS

The body needs these chemical elements in small amounts to ensure proper growth and functioning. They include all the vitamins and minerals. The traditional keto diet may lead to a deficiency in vitamins and minerals due to its reduced consumption of fruits and vegetables. Still, the keto Mediterranean version is vitamin-rich, ensuring that you always have a complete mix.

VITAMINS

Vitamins can be water soluble or fat soluble. Water-soluble vitamins include folic acid, niacin, thiamin, and vitamins B6, B12, and C. They are necessary for the production of energy and for building cells. Fat-soluble vitamins include vitamins A, D, E, and K. They help repair tissue, maintain good vision, and build bones.

MINERALS

Most of our bones are composed of minerals, including calcium and phosphate. For everything your body does, at least one mineral is required. When your body is in ketosis, your liver removes sodium at an increased rate, affecting potassium levels in your body. Your body is always trying to have a particular sodium-to-potassium ratio. Since the body cannot produce sodium, you must increase your sodium intake while on the keto Mediterranean diet to maintain the necessary ratio.

Now that you better understand how many benefits can be derived from combining Mediterranean and keto diets, I'm sure you can't wait to start. The following section will guide you through getting started on your keto Mediterranean journey, including what to eat and what ingredients are the most essential.

GETTING STARTED

Before listing what foods you should and should not eat on this diet, let's take a moment to **talk about buying your food.** Try to opt for fruits and vegetables that are fresh and in season. This will ensure that you get the most nutrients out of them. If you can't get fresh produce, then your next best option is flash-frozen foods. These foods retain most of their original nutrient content. Canned fruits and vegetables should be a last resort since they lose most of their nutritional value and have added preservatives.

When purchasing protein, try to find local producers. This way, you will have a better idea of how the animal was raised, and you may even be able to get better cuts. If you're buying protein from the supermarket, try to ensure it is hormone- and antibiotic-free.

The best advice I can give you when **making significant lifestyle and dietary changes is just to start.** Even if you only start with one meal daily, that's okay. Slowly, you make more and more swaps for healthier, more wholesome options. Here are just a few tips and tricks to guide you as you start:

- It's never all or nothing. You can take your time and make changes at your own pace. You definitely don't have to give up everything that you love.

- Don't feel guilty about eating something that's not on the list. Cut yourself some slack, and don't dwell on it.

- Take the time to listen to your body and what it truly needs. Eat when you're hungry, not when you're bored.

- There may be days that you're ravenous, and your body needs more carbohydrates. That's okay. Every day is going to be different.

- Don't eat it if you don't like it! Pick foods you enjoy eating or won't stick to the diet.

- Always check with your healthcare provider before changing your diet and lifestyle.

- Most importantly, have fun! Try new fruits and vegetables that appeal to you. Remember, this is a holistic approach to dieting. The more pleasure you derive from all aspects of the process, the more likely you will stick with it.

KETO MEDITERRANEAN DIET STAPLES

On the keto Mediterranean diet, your plate should be filled with non-starchy vegetables, which will usually be cooked in fat, and you should always have a source of protein at every meal. Once you get used to what you can and cannot eat, mixing and matching the ingredients to suit your personal preferences will become much easier. To start, here are a few staples that should always be in your pantry:

- *Extra-virgin olive oil:* This heart-healthy oil is loaded with monounsaturated and polyunsaturated fats and is essential to all Mediterranean cooking. Not to mention, it has no cholesterol.

- *Vegetables:* Almost one half of your plate should comprise low-carb vegetables in a variety of colors. The more colorful your vegetables, the more nutrients they contain. Opt for vegetables that are in season and that you enjoy eating.

- *Fruits:* These are high in fiber and loaded with nutrients. Just be sure to choose ones that are also low in carbohydrates. Try to use fresh fruits as much as possible, and if you do have dried fruits, opt for those with no added sugar. Also, dried fruits tend to be higher in carbohydrates than fresh fruits.

- *Nuts and seeds:* These are a great source of plant-based protein, fiber, and potassium. You can have them alone or use them as a garnish for salads and yogurt.

- *Poultry and eggs:* You can enjoy poultry a few times a week and have eggs daily if you like. They're both excellent sources of protein.

- *Seafood:* A great source of omega-3 fatty acids, seafood is crucial for brain and heart health. Opt for seafood that you enjoy eating, and that fits your budget.

- *Dairy:* Yogurt and cheese can be had in small amounts on a daily basis.

- *Red meat:* You can enjoy red meat occasionally but try to choose leaner cuts that are less processed for a healthier option.

- *Herbs and spices:* A few herbs and spices can make any dish flavorful and appealing. Half the fun in cooking is adding flavor to the ingredients.

FOODS TO ENJOY

- *Low-carb fruits:* lemons, blueberries, avocados, strawberries, olives, and cantaloupes

- *Nuts and seeds:* hazelnuts, pistachios, almonds, walnuts, chia seeds, pumpkin seeds, and pecans

- *Non-starchy vegetables:* tomatoes, cauliflower, broccoli, zucchini, salad greens, cucumbers, okra, eggplant, mushrooms, kale, cabbage, and Brussels sprouts

- *Proteins:* all fish, seafood, eggs, and poultry

- *Fats:* olive oil and avocado oil

- *Herbs and spices:* garlic, ginger, turmeric, thyme, oregano, sage, cinnamon, cloves, cilantro, cumin, basil, cardamom, rosemary, mint, black pepper, paprika, and chili powder

- *Dairy:* Greek yogurt, feta cheese, goat cheese, and parmesan cheese

FOODS TO EAT IN MODERATION

- *Red meat:* lamb, beef, and pork

- *High-fat dairy:* heavy cream, hard cheeses, and full-fat yogurt

- *High-fat oils:* butter, ghee, and coconut oil

FOODS TO AVOID

- *Grains:* rice, cereal, pasta, corn, and wheat products

- *High-carb fruits:* oranges, bananas, mangoes, peaches, plums, and apples

- *High-carb vegetables:* yams and potatoes

- *Sugars:* maple syrup, honey, and agave

- *Processed foods:* deli meats, hot dogs, snacks, and soda

Now that you have the basics, I hope you can start cooking. All the recipes are easy to follow and use readily available ingredients. Let's get started!

BREAKFASTS

BREAKFASTS

Servings: 4

Prep Time: 10 minutes

Cook Time: 20 minutes

MUSHROOM FRITTATA WITH PARMESAN

When I describe Mediterranean cuisine, I say it is an elegant cuisine for every day. It's a cuisine that never gets boring: on a busy Monday morning, on a holiday weekend, on a rainy Wednesday, on Christmas or a birthday... This cuisine has all the dishes you could need. There are dishes to suit every diet, including keto. Meet one of the most popular and wholesome breakfast dishes — the French omelet or Italian frittata.

INGREDIENTS:

- 4 medium eggs
- 3 Tbsp. heavy cream
- 1/3 cup (40 g) feta cheese, crumbled
- 4 cremini mushrooms, sliced
- 2 white onions, diced

- 4 Tbsp. baby spinach, chopped
- 2 scallions, roughly chopped
- 1/3 cup (20 g) parmesan, grated
- sea salt and ground black peppercorns, to taste

PROCESS:

1. Preheat your oven to 400°F (205°C).
2. Whisk heavy cream together with eggs, salt, and pepper. Mix in vegetables and feta cheese.
3. Spray a baking pan with olive oil.
4. Pour the frittata mixture into the baking pan and sprinkle with grated Parmesan.
5. Cook in the preheated oven for 15-20 minutes.
6. Serve with crispy keto ciabatta.

NUTRITION FACTS (Per Serving)

Calories: 181, Net Carbs: 6.4 g, Total Carbohydrates: 7.9 g, Total Fat: 12.4 g, Cholesterol 194 mg, Sodium 258 mg, Protein: 10.5 g, Fiber: 1.5 g, Sugar: 3.7 g

BREAKFASTS

Servings: 6 slices

Prep Time: 10 minutes

Cook Time: 20 minutes

ASPARAGUS FRITTATA

Another feature of Mediterranean cuisine is the recognizability of the ingredients. Ingredients are not chopped, processed, or blended to the point that you can no longer tell what they are. We try to emphasize the flavor of each ingredient, not alter it beyond recognition. Of course, this approach demands fresh, high-quality ingredients. This dish incorporates fresh, juicy, seasonal asparagus, organic eggs, and feta cheese.

INGREDIENTS:

- 1 Tbsp. (14 g) unsalted butter
- 1 small white onion (50 g), chopped
- 2 garlic cloves, minced
- 4 large whole eggs
- 1¼ cups (300 ml) heavy cream

- ¼ tsp dried oregano
- ⅛ tsp dried red pepper flakes
- Sea salt, to taste
- 4 oz. (110 g) feta cheese (crumbled)
- 10 oz. (285 g) asparagus

PROCESS:

1. Preheat the oven to 325°F (163°C) and lightly grease a 9-inch round baking pan.

2. On medium-low heat, melt the butter in a frying pan. Add chopped onions and garlic. Cook for 5 minutes until translucent (not golden).

3. Transfer the onion and garlic mixture to the baking pan. Sprinkle crumbled feta on the top.

4. Arrange asparagus in a single layer in the pan.

5. Whisk eggs in a medium-sized bowl. Add the cream, oregano, red pepper flakes, and sea salt and whisk until fully incorporated.

6. Pour the egg mixture over the ingredients in the baking pan.

7. Bake for 15-20 minutes until the frittata is set and lightly golden along the edges.

8. Sprinkle with chopped fresh dill.

NUTRITION FACTS (Per Serving)

Calories: 305, Net Carbs: 4.4 g, Total Carbohydrates: 5.7 g, Total Fat: 28.4 g, Cholesterol 215 mg, Sodium 292 mg, Protein: 9.5 g, Fiber: 1.3 g, Sugar: 2.7 g

BREAKFASTS

Servings: 8

Prep Time: 15 minutes

Cook Time: 55 minutes

CHICKEN CASSEROLE

Mediterranean cuisine has its own cooking rules, which are helpful for all home cooks. The dishes are not difficult to prepare, but following the rules leads to quality results and exquisite meals. The first rule is to take the meat out of the fridge an hour before cooking it. In other words: do not cook cold meat. When you fry the meat in a pan, put it into the hot oil. And never serve meat immediately after cooking. Allow it to stand for a while. For chicken, it's about 10 minutes.

INGREDIENTS:

- 1 lb. (450 g) turkey/chicken fillets, diced
- 1 white onion (70 g), chopped
- 10 oz. (280 g) broccoli florets
- 1 cup (250 ml) whole milk
- 6 slices of keto bread, cut into bite-sized pieces

- 1 cup (116 g) bell peppers, chopped
- 1 can (14 oz./400 g) artichoke hearts, drained
- ½ cup (60 g) feta cheese, crumbled
- 8 whole eggs
- ½ tsp. kosher salt
- 2 tbsp. olive oil

PROCESS:

1. Preheat your oven to 350°F (180°C).
2. Heat olive oil in a large skillet over medium-high heat. Add chicken pieces and cook for 8 minutes, stirring occasionally. Add chopped onion and salt to the skillet. Cook for an additional 5 minutes.
3. Beat eggs and milk together in a bowl.
4. Spray a baking dish with cooking spray.
5. Transfer the ingredients from the skillet to the baking dish. Add chopped vegetables, crumbled feta, and bread pieces. Pour the milk-egg mixture over them.
6. Bake the casserole in the preheated oven for 35-45 minutes.
7. Remove from the oven and let it sit for 10 minutes before serving.

NUTRITION FACTS (Per Serving)

Calories: 311, Net Carbs: 6.5 g, Total Carbohydrates: 12 g, Total Fat: 15.1 g, Cholesterol 223 mg, Sodium 353 mg, Protein: 29.5 g, Fiber: 5.5 g, Sugar: 3.7 g

BREAKFASTS

Servings: 2

Prep Time: 10 minutes

GREEK SALAD

This is an easy-to-make, classic Mediterranean dish that does not require rare or expensive ingredients and is not time-consuming. Make this dish using your favorite ingredients or even leftovers from the fridge. Use fat bombs as a protein and fat base and arrange them with vegetables and a nutritious sauce. Create your own composition and remember the rule of Mediterranean cooking: limiting the number of ingredients is better than including the wrong ones.

INGREDIENTS:

- 2 cucumbers, sliced
- 1 red onion (70 g), diced
- 6 cherry tomatoes, halved
- 1 tsp. Italian seasoning
- 12 black olives
- 6 oz. (170 g) mozzarella cheese, cubed

- lettuce leaves
- 2 Tbsp. tahini dressing
- 2 Tbsp. sunflower seeds, roasted
- sea salt
- extra virgin olive oil

PROCESS:

1. Assemble the bowl. Add diced cucumber, tomato halves, lettuce leaves, onion rings, mozzarella cubes, olives, and sunflower seeds. Drizzle with tahini dressing.

2. Serve fresh with grilled chicken slices and poached egg.

NUTRITION FACTS (Per Serving)

Calories: 360, Net Carbs: 12.5 g, Total Carbohydrates: 19 g, Total Fat: 24.7 g, Cholesterol 14 mg, Sodium 414 mg, Protein: 13.5 g, Fiber: 6.5 g, Sugar: 10.7 g

BREAKFASTS

Servings: 4

Prep Time: 10 minutes

Cook Time: 25 minutes

SICILIAN CAPONATA

Caponata is a versatile Sicilian dish whose main ingredient is chopped aubergine (eggplant). It is very similar to a vegetable stew with the addition of raisins, nuts, and honey, but we avoid them on the keto diet. It is important to choose seasonal organic vegetables, preferably those traditionally used in Italian, Spanish, or Greek cuisine. When choosing vegetables, focus not on appearance but on flavor and texture.

When you salt the eggplant, leave it to stand in a colander for a while to draw off any bitterness. Do not serve the caponata immediately after cooking — let it rest for 40-50 minutes.

INGREDIENTS:

- 1 eggplant (1½ lb./675 g), cubed
- 1 red onion (70 g), chopped
- 1 bell pepper (150 g), chopped
- 2 medium tomatoes, peeled and chopped
- 1 celery stalk, diced
- sea salt, black pepper
- 2 Tbsp. capers

- 1 Tbsp. pine nuts
- 3 Tbsp. olives, diced
- ¼ tsp. red pepper flakes
- ¼ cup (60 ml) red wine vinegar
- ¼ cup fresh Italian herbs, chopped
- olive oil

PROCESS:

1. Preheat your oven to 400°F (205°C).
2. Season eggplant cubes with salt and pepper and drizzle with some olive oil. Roast in a preheated oven for 20-25 minutes until golden brown, tossing twice during the process.
3. Heat 1 tablespoon of olive oil in a frying pan and add chopped onion, bell peppers, celery, salt, and pepper. Cook for 5 minutes until softened.
4. Add tomatoes, capers, olives, pine nuts, vinegar, and red pepper flakes. Cook, while stirring, for an additional 7-8 minutes.
5. Add the roasted eggplant and chopped herbs and cook for another 5 minutes.
6. Serve as a topping over a keto baguette or ciabatta.

NUTRITION FACTS (Per Serving)

Calories: 160, Net Carbs: 7.8 g, Total Carbohydrates: 16 g, Total Fat: 9.7 g, Cholesterol 0 mg, Sodium 195 mg, Protein: 3.5 g, Fiber: 8.2 g, Sugar: 9.7 g

BREAKFASTS

Servings: 8 muffins

Prep Time: 10 minutes

Cook Time: 20 minutes

EGG MUFFINS

Try substituting the chicken and broccoli with mushrooms, grated cheddar, spinach, bell peppers, and/ or tomatoes. These resemble my favorite frittata but are so cute and easy to eat. They store well in the fridge, too.

INGREDIENTS:

* 6 large eggs
* 2 Tbsp. heavy cream
* 2 cups (180 g) broccoli florets
* 1 small yellow onion (60 g), chopped

* 3 oz. (85 g) turkey/chicken fillets, cooked and chopped
* 4 oz. (110 g) feta, crumbled
* ¼ tsp. smoked paprika
* kosher salt, and black pepper to taste

PROCESS:

1. Whisk eggs, heavy cream, salt, pepper, and paprika together in a bowl.
2. Combine the egg mixture with the remaining ingredients.
3. Preheat your oven to 350°F (180°C). Spray muffin molds with olive oil.
4. Pour the muffin mixture into the molds. Bake for 15-20 minutes or until set.
5. Let them cool slightly before serving.

NUTRITION FACTS (Per Serving)

Calories: 134, Net Carbs: 2.5 g, Total Carbohydrates: 3.3 g, Total Fat: 8.7 g, Cholesterol 166 mg, Sodium 224 mg, Protein: 10.5 g, Fiber: 0.8 g, Sugar: 1.7 g

BREAKFASTS

Servings: 4

Prep Time: 10 minutes

MEDITERRANEAN BREAKFAST TOAST

I lived in Italy and France for several years. First, I studied at the Culinary Arts School, then I interned at various restaurants. But in all my travels, I was invariably accompanied by breakfasts of crispy toast. I would experiment with toppings, but I always gravitated to seasonal vegetables with minimal processing, cheeses, and sausages from the local region. It seemed to me that, in this way, I got to know better the cuisine I love with all my soul, which I generously share with you.

INGREDIENTS:

- 4 keto bread slices, toasted

FOR THE TOPPINGS:
- 4 cherry tomatoes, halved
- 8 oz. (230 g) mozzarella, cubed
- 1 tsp. red pepper flakes, crushed
- ½ cup fresh basil leaves
- 1 tsp. olive oil

PROCESS:

1. Arrange all the toppings on the bread slices and sprinkle with red pepper flakes and olive oil.

NUTRITION FACTS (Per Serving)

Calories: 124, Net Carbs: 8.8 g, Total Carbohydrates: 10.3 g, Total Fat: 4.7 g, Cholesterol 9 mg, Sodium 224 mg, Protein: 9.5 g, Fiber: 3.5 g, Sugar: 3.2 g

BREAKFASTS

Servings: 6

Prep Time: 10 minutes

Cook Time: 20 minutes

WHOLESOME GRANOLA

Granola originated in the late 19th century in the US. But by now, it has become so ingrained in Italy and the Middle East that we consider it a Mediterranean dish. Crunchy granola is served for breakfast with yogurt, as a snack on hikes, and as a topping sprinkled over pastries and ice cream. For variety, you can add fresh berries and fruits to it. It's also high in calories and will keep you full all day.

INGREDIENTS:

- ⅓ cup (50 g) almonds
- ¾ cup (100 g) Brazil nuts
- 1 tsp. cinnamon
- 4 Tbsp. cocoa or cacao nibs
- ¼ cup (60 g) coconut oil, melted
- ⅓ cup (50 g) walnuts

- ½ cup (60 g) pecans
- ½ cup (50 g) pumpkin seeds
- pinch of salt
- ¾ cup (130 g) sunflower seeds
- 4 Tbsp. toasted coconut flakes
- ¼ cup (60 ml) water

PROCESS:

1. Preheat oven to 350°F (180°C).
2. Add almonds, Brazil nuts, walnuts, pecans, pumpkin seeds, and sunflower seeds to a blender or food processor and pulse a few times to break up the nuts a bit.
3. Transfer the nuts to a mixing bowl.
4. Add cinnamon, toasted cocoa nibs, coconut chips, and a pinch of salt. Stir to combine all of the ingredients thoroughly.
5. Pour the melted coconut butter over the nuts and add water. Coat the nuts thoroughly.
6. Spread the entire mixture evenly onto a baking sheet.
7. Bake for 15-20 minutes, stirring the granola twice.
8. Remove the baking sheet from the oven and let the granola cool completely.
9. Serve with yogurt, a berry smoothie, or full-fat milk.

NUTRITION FACTS (Per Serving)

Calories: 546, Net Carbs: 13.8 g, Total Carbohydrates: 21.3 g, Total Fat: 50 g, Cholesterol 0 mg, Sodium 4 mg, Protein: 11.5 g, Fiber: 7.5 g, Sugar: 10.2 g

BREAKFASTS

Servings: 4 crepes

Prep Time: 10 minutes

Cook Time: 10 minutes

FRENCH KETO CREPES

Sunday mornings around here start with fragrant crepes and strawberry jam. Eating them goes much quicker than cooking them! My family eats them right out of the frying pan. That's the best way, according to the Mummy Trolls: cold crepes lose out to their hot counterparts. I get it, and I try to grab a couple for myself while they are piping hot.

INGREDIENTS:

- ¼ cup (30 g) almond flour
- 4 whole eggs
- 1 tsp. vanilla extract

- 1 Tbsp. coconut oil
- ¼ tsp. ground cinnamon
- 1 Tbsp. sweetener of your choice

PROCESS:

1. Preheat a non-stick frying pan. Grease the preheated pan with coconut oil.

2. Whisk together almond flour, eggs, vanilla, cinnamon, and sweetener in a large bowl.

3. Spoon the batter into the pan using a ¼ measuring cup. Tilt the pan to spread the batter evenly across the bottom.

4. Set the pan flat over the heat and cook until the edges of the crepe start to crisp up.

5. Using a rubber spatula, loosen the crepe from the pan and flip the crepe over with one fluid motion. Cook the crepe on the second side for 1-2 minutes before transferring it to a plate.

6. Serve warm with coconut whipped cream and berry jam.

NUTRITION FACTS (Per Serving)

Calories: 126, Net Carbs: 1.6 g, Total Carbohydrates: 2.7 g, Total Fat: 10.2 g, Cholesterol 164 mg, Sodium 63 mg, Protein: 6.5 g, Fiber: 1.1 g, Sugar: 0.5 g

Servings: 1 flatbread

Prep Time: 5 minutes

Cook Time: 5 minutes

SPINACH WRAP

INGREDIENTS:

- 2 Tbsp. flaxseed meal
- 1 whole egg
- ¼ cup (15 g) fresh spinach
- ¼ tsp. garlic powder
- ¼ tsp. baking powder
- 1 Tbsp. water

PROCESS:

1. Grease an 8-inch glass baking dish with oil spray.
2. In a food processor, combine egg, spinach, water, flaxseed meal, garlic powder, and baking powder.
3. Transfer the mixture to the baking dish, ensuring a uniform and smooth texture.
4. Place the dish in the microwave and microwave on high for 3-4 minutes.
5. Remove from the oven and let it stand for 2 minutes.
6. Serve with scrambled egg and avocado, or choose your favorite filling.

NUTRITION FACTS (Per Serving)

Calories: 144, Net Carbs: 1.8 g, Total Carbohydrates: 6 g, Total Fat: 8.9 g, Cholesterol 164 mg, Sodium 79 mg, Protein: 8.7 g, Fiber: 4.2 g, Sugar: 0.8 g

SNACKS

SNACKS

Servings: 16 falafels

Prep Time: 10 minutes

Cook Time: 20 minutes

CAULIFLOWER FALAFEL

Falafel is one of the most delicious kinds of fast food. I brought its recipe back from the Middle East. Traditionally, it is made from chickpeas or another kind of bean, but for the keto diet, I replaced the main ingredient with a more keto-friendly one. You can tell it's a very different dish from the original, but our keto falafels are just as delicious — and they make the perfect snack. They can be baked in the oven or an air fryer.

These work great as a pita filling with a vegetable salad or as a snack with tahini sauce.

INGREDIENTS:

- 1 Tbsp. avocado oil
- 1 cup (130 g) celery stalks, chopped
- 1 Tbsp. chia seeds
- ½ tsp. ground paprika
- ¼ cup (25 g) coconut flour/almond flour
- 1 tsp. ground cumin
- 1 Tbsp. onion flakes
- ½ cup cilantro leaves, finely chopped
- 4 garlic cloves, minced
- 2 cups (215 g) cauliflower rice
- sea salt
- 2½ Tbsp. water

PROCESS:

1. Preheat the oven to 350⁰F (180⁰C).
2. Mix the cauliflower, celery, coconut flour, minced garlic, paprika, dried onion, avocado oil, and salt in a large bowl.
3. Add chia seeds and water and stir until the mixture achieves a dough-like consistency.
4. Pull off a walnut-sized piece of dough and roll it into a ball between greased palms.
5. Place the falafel balls on a greased baking sheet.
6. Bake the falafels for 15-20 minutes until lightly brown.

NUTRITION FACTS (Per Serving)

Calories: 20, Net Carbs: 1.5 g, Total Carbohydrates: 3.1 g, Total Fat: 0.9 g, Cholesterol 0 mg, Sodium 11 mg, Protein: 0.7 g, Fiber: 1.6 g, Sugar: 0.6 g

SNACKS

Servings: 1 cup

Prep Time: 4 minutes

Cook Time: 12 minutes

ROASTED NUTS

Nuts and seeds are the healthiest snacks for followers of the Mediterranean lifestyle — and keto followers especially — because they are indispensable sources of unsaturated plant-based fats. Of course, raw nuts are delicious, but I recommend you roast them with spices. You will find that their flavor becomes even brighter and richer.

You can eat them on their own or add them to various meat and fish dishes, salads, and soups. Doing so will add a nutritious, buttery flavor and a lot of nutrients.

INGREDIENTS:

- 1 cup (130 g) raw almonds/pecans/walnuts/hazelnuts
- 1 tsp. coconut oil, melted

FOR SWEET NUTS (optional):
- granulated sweetener
- cinnamon
- pumpkin pie spice

FOR SAVORY NUTS (optional):
- herbs
- nutmeg
- oriental spices/curry
- onion/garlic powder
- chili powder
- olive oil/melted butter/coconut oil

PROCESS:

1. Preheat your oven to 350°F (180°C).
2. In a small bowl, combine nuts with your favorite seasoning.
3. Line a baking sheet with parchment paper.
4. Arrange the nuts in a single layer on the baking sheet and bake for 8-12 minutes until fragrant.
5. Cool completely before serving.
6. Roasted nuts can be stored in an airtight container for up to 3 weeks.

NUTRITION FACTS (Per Serving)

Calories: 790, Net Carbs: 11.3 g, Total Carbohydrates: 27.9 g, Total Fat: 69.9 g, Cholesterol 0 mg, Sodium 1 mg, Protein: 27.7 g, Fiber: 16.6 g, Sugar: 5.6 g

Servings: 2

Prep Time: 5 minutes

Cook Time: 6 minutes

TOAST WITH CHEESE AND HAM

INGREDIENTS:

- 2 slices of keto Italian bread
- 1 tsp. unsalted butter
- 2 slices of cheddar/blue cheese
- 2 slices of Parma ham
- 3 red onion rings
- 2 slices of Roma tomato
- 1 whole egg, cooked

PROCESS:

1. Heat a skillet over medium heat. Butter one side of both slices of bread and place them butter-side down on the skillet.

2. Add cheese, ham slices, onion rings, and tomato slices to one slice of bread and place the other slice of bread on top.

3. Grill on both sides until the cheese has melted.

4. Serve with fried eggs and fresh summer salad.

NUTRITION FACTS (Per Serving)

Calories: 257, Net Carbs: 18.5 g, Total Carbohydrates: 25.1 g, Total Fat: 9.2 g, Cholesterol 109 mg, Sodium 709 mg, Protein: 20.3 g, Fiber: 6.6 g, Sugar: 7.8 g

Servings: 4

Prep Time: 10 minutes

Cook Time: 40 minutes

BABA GANOUSH

Baba ganoush came to us from the Middle East and is very popular on the keto menu. This fantastic creamy dip is very quick and easy to make. The main ingredient is eggplant, which would traditionally be cooked over an open fire. You can grill it or roast it in the oven. It has many variations based on the spices used (try cumin, chili, or red pepper flakes), and sometimes the eggplant is replaced with zucchini.

Baba ganoush is an excellent snack with flatbread or fresh sliced vegetables.

INGREDIENTS:

- 1 medium eggplant (1 lb./450 g)
- 1 Tbsp. vegetable oil
- 2 Tbsp. tahini paste
- 2 tsp. fresh lemon juice
- 2 garlic cloves, peeled

- ⅛ tsp. kosher salt
- ⅛ tsp. ground nutmeg
- ½ tsp. smoked paprika

PROCESS:

1. Preheat your oven to 425°F (220°C).
2. Wrap the garlic in aluminum foil.
3. Use a fork to poke several holes in the skin of the eggplant, and then wrap it in aluminum foil as well.
4. Roast the garlic in the preheated oven for 15 minutes and the eggplant for 40 minutes.
5. When it is cool enough to handle, peel and chop the eggplant. Let it drain for 5 minutes.
6. Put the drained eggplant with all other ingredients (except the paprika) into the food processor and pulse until you have a coarse puree.
7. Transfer to a serving bowl and sprinkle with smoked paprika. Serve with keto pita bread.

NUTRITION FACTS (Per Serving)

Calories: 107, Net Carbs: 4.4 g, Total Carbohydrates: 9 g, Total Fat: 7.7 g, Cholesterol 0 mg, Sodium 12 mg, Protein: 2.3 g, Fiber: 4.6 g, Sugar: 3.8 g

Servings: 4

Prep Time: 10 minutes

Cook Time: 10 minutes

GRILLED PORTOBELLO MUSHROOMS

Portobello is a common name for the mushrooms we know so well. You can take button mushrooms, champignons, white/brown mushrooms, cremini, baby bella, etc. They are all great for marinating and grilling. The mushrooms are very nutritious, low-carb, and an excellent source of riboflavin, which makes them popular among keto followers.

I recommend pairing them with grilled vegetables and blue cheese/feta.

INGREDIENTS:

* 3 Tbsp. balsamic vinegar
* ½ tsp. onion powder
* 2 Tbsp. avocado oil
* 4 large Portobello mushrooms
* 1-2 tsp. liquid smoke
* 1 garlic clove, minced
* kosher salt, ground pepper
* 3 Tbsp. soy sauce
* 1 Tbsp. Worcestershire sauce

PROCESS:

1. Remove the stems from the mushrooms.
2. Combine all ingredients for the marinade (except the mushrooms and oil) in a bowl and mix well.
3. Add the mushrooms to the marinade and let them sit for 20 minutes.
4. Heat a grill or frying pan to medium-high heat.
5. Brush the cooking surface with oil and arrange the mushrooms evenly in one layer. Cook for 5 minutes on each side.
6. You can serve them as an appetizer or assemble them in a sandwich.

NUTRITION FACTS (Per Serving)

Calories: 49, Net Carbs: 4.8 g, Total Carbohydrates: 6.4 g, Total Fat: 0.7 g, Cholesterol 0 mg, Sodium 719 mg, Protein: 4.7 g, Fiber: 1.6 g, Sugar: 1.1 g

Servings: 16 mushrooms

Prep Time: 10 minutes

Cook Time: 25 minutes

STUFFED MUSHROOMS

There is no doubt that mushrooms are delicious on their own. But if we stuff them, we get a completely different dish and a delicious appetizer. The ingredients for stuffing can be chosen from cheeses, spicy vegetables, herbs, or ground meat. We choose mushrooms with a large round cap, where you can put a lot of stuffing in a basket. The stalk is sliced and mixed with the rest of the stuffing ingredients.

INGREDIENTS:

- 16 button mushrooms (1 lb./450 g), rinsed and dried
- ¼ cup (60 g) sun-dried tomatoes, chopped
- ½ cup (75 g) keto breadcrumbs
- 1 green onion, chopped
- 4 oz. (110 g) cream cheese
- 4 oz. (110 g) parmesan, shredded
- ½ tsp. red pepper flakes

PROCESS:

1. Remove the stems from the mushrooms and scoop out the center. Chop them finely.
2. Combine the chopped stems, sun-dried tomatoes, breadcrumbs, cream cheese, shredded cheese, red pepper flakes, and green onion, and mix well.
3. Fill the mushroom caps with the stuffing.
4. Preheat your oven to 400°F (205°C). Line a baking dish with parchment paper and grease with olive oil.
5. Arrange mushrooms in a single layer in the baking dish. Sprinkle with shredded cheese and olive oil. Cook for 25 minutes.
6. Your perfect Mediterranean appetizer is ready.

NUTRITION FACTS (Per Serving)

Calories: 62, Net Carbs: 2.3 g, Total Carbohydrates: 2.9 g, Total Fat: 4.1 g, Cholesterol 12 mg, Sodium 109 mg, Protein: 4.4 g, Fiber: 0.6 g, Sugar: 0.6 g

MEAT & POULTRY

MEAT & POULTRY

Servings: 8

Prep Time: 10 minutes (plus 1-2 hours for marinating)

Cook Time: 7-10 minutes

GREEK CHICKEN SOUVLAKI

Traditionally, souvlaki is made from pork, beef, or lamb, but I offer you the chicken fillet option. We marinate the poultry to give it a spicy flavor and keep it juicy inside. If you grill a chicken fillet without marinating it first, it will become dry and tough.

Souvlaki is usually eaten as a pita sandwich with a fresh salad.

INGREDIENTS:

- 2 lb. (900 g) chicken fillets, cut into 2" cubes
- 1 Tbsp. dried oregano
- 2 Tbsp. olive oil
- 4 garlic cloves, minced
- 1 tsp. kosher salt
- 1 tsp. smoked paprika
- ½ tsp. ground black pepper
- ¼ tsp. red pepper flakes
- ½ lime juice

PROCESS:

1. Combine olive oil, lime juice, herbs, spices, salt, and minced garlic.
2. Marinate chicken pieces in the spice and lime juice mixture for 30-90 minutes.
3. Thread the chicken pieces onto skewers.
4. Preheat your grill.
5. Arrange the skewers on the grill and cook until golden brown, flipping the skewers from time to time.
6. Serve souvlaki with grilled keto pita bread and tomato sauce.

NUTRITION FACTS (Per Serving)

Calories: 249, Net Carbs: 0.7 g, Total Carbohydrates: 1.1 g, Total Fat: 12 g, Cholesterol 100 mg, Sodium 97 mg, Protein: 32.4 g, Fiber: 0.4 g, Sugar: 0.1 g

Servings: 4

Prep Time: 8 minutes

Cook Time: 30 minutes

CREAMY CHICKEN STEW

Chicken fillets go very well with heavy cream, which allows the chicken to stay juicy and tender. We add vegetables, spinach, and spices to the cream sauce. Tomato paste, crushed tomatoes, or curry can also be added. The sun-dried tomatoes can be replaced with mushrooms.

I recommend asparagus or broccoli as a side dish.

INGREDIENTS:

- 4 chicken breasts
- 4 Tbsp. salted butter
- 4 oz. (110 g) sun-dried tomatoes, diced
- 4 oz. (110 g) fresh spinach, chopped
- 4 oz. (110 g) parmesan, grated

- 1 cup (250 ml) heavy cream
- 2 garlic cloves, crushed
- kosher salt and ground black pepper
- olive oil

PROCESS:

1. Preheat olive oil in the frying pan.
2. Season chicken breasts with salt and pepper. Fry them in the pan for 10 minutes or until golden brown, flipping halfway through.
3. Melt the butter in a skillet. Add chopped sun-dried tomatoes and crushed garlic and sauté for 5-7 minutes.
4. Add spinach and continue to cook, stirring occasionally. Add heavy cream and shredded Parmesan.
5. Submerge the cooked chicken breasts in the sauce and let them simmer gently for 10 minutes.
6. Serve with fresh salad, grilled vegetables, or crusty keto bread

NUTRITION FACTS (Per Serving)

Calories: 682, Net Carbs: 4.3 g, Total Carbohydrates: 5.3 g, Total Fat: 52.4 g, Cholesterol 249 mg, Sodium 474 mg, Protein: 48.4 g, Fiber: 1 g, Sugar: 0.9 g

MEAT & POULTRY

Servings: 4

Prep Time: 10 minutes (½ - 2 hours for marinating)

Cook Time: 60 minutes

GREEK CHICKEN WITH LEMONS

These spicy chicken thighs are easy to make and great for weeknight dinners. I recommend coating the chicken with a lemon-spice marinade before roasting. It will make the meat tender, flavorful, and juicy. Rosemary sprigs can be fresh or dried.

These citrus chicken thighs will also be good the next day. Remove all the lemon slices before refrigerating so they do not become bitter.

INGREDIENTS:

- 4 chicken thighs, bone-in and skin-on
- ½ lemon, juiced
- ½ lemon, sliced
- 1 Tbsp. dried rosemary
- ½ tsp. red pepper flakes
- ½ tsp. onion powder
- 4 garlic cloves, crushed
- a pinch of sea salt and black pepper
- 2 Tbsp. olive oil

PROCESS:

1. Combine olive oil, lemon juice, rosemary, onion powder, red pepper flakes, salt, and pepper. Brush over the chicken thighs and let them marinate for at least 1 hour.

2. Preheat your oven to 400°F (205°C).

3. Arrange chicken thighs in a baking dish. Pour the extra marinade over the chicken. Top with lemon slices and rosemary sprigs.

4. Bake for 50-60 minutes.

5. Serve with cauliflower rice or keto garlic bread.

NUTRITION FACTS (Per Serving)

Calories: 297, Net Carbs: 3.1 g, Total Carbohydrates: 4.1 g, Total Fat: 23.4 g, Cholesterol 90 mg, Sodium 174 mg, Protein: 18.4 g, Fiber: 1 g, Sugar: 1.9 g

MEAT
& POULTRY

STUFFED CHICKEN BREAST

Stuffed chicken breast is good because of its tasty filling and keeps the meat juicy and tender. Of course, you can keep leftovers in the refrigerator and reheat them later, but remember: the meat will get a little tougher when you reheat it. Therefore, try to serve this mouth-watering dish fresh and warm.

Grilled vegetables such as asparagus and broccoli are a perfect accompaniment.

INGREDIENTS:

- 2 large chicken breasts
- 4 oz. (110 g) mozzarella/feta cheese, shredded
- 4 sun-dried tomatoes, chopped
- 8 black olives, diced
- 1 Tbsp. oregano
- kosher salt, black pepper, paprika
- olive oil

PROCESS:

1. Carefully cut the chicken breasts horizontally, making a pocket.
2. Combine shredded mozzarella, sun-dried tomatoes, chopped olives, oregano, salt, and pepper.
3. Fill the chicken pockets with mozzarella stuffing. Spray the outside of the chicken breasts with olive oil and season with salt, paprika, and pepper.
4. Place a skillet over medium heat and add olive oil.
5. Fry the stuffed chicken breasts on each side until brown.

NUTRITION FACTS (Per Serving)

Calories: 582, Net Carbs: 8.3 g, Total Carbohydrates: 12.7 g, Total Fat: 32.9 g, Cholesterol 171 mg, Sodium 416 mg, Protein: 59.4 g, Fiber: 4.5 g, Sugar: 6.6 g

MEAT & POULTRY

Servings: 4

Prep Time: 10 minutes

Cook Time: 30 minutes

CHICKEN STEW WITH VEGETABLES

Vegetables have a place of honor in traditional Mediterranean cuisine, which is part of the reason the people live so long. The different climatic conditions of the region contribute to the diversity of the vegetables. The Mediterranean diet embraces asparagus, pumpkin, broccoli, tomatoes, and an infinite variety of other vegetables, baked, boiled, grilled, roasted, or stuffed.

You can experiment with your favorite vegetables in this stew, customizing the dish and making it more nutritious and delicious.

INGREDIENTS:

- 1 lb. (450 g) chicken fillets, chopped
- 1 can (14 oz./400 g) artichoke hearts, drained
- 4 ripe tomatoes, chopped
- 1 white onion (70 g), diced
- 2 garlic cloves, minced
- 1 red bell pepper (150 g), chopped
- 3 tbsp. herbs de Provence
- sea salt and black pepper

PROCESS:

1. Heat a cast-iron skillet over medium heat.
2. Add chicken fillets, and cook for 10-15 minutes until lightly browned.
3. Add garlic and onion and sauté for 5 minutes, stirring often.
4. Add herbs de Provence, artichoke hearts, chopped bell peppers, and tomatoes, and cook for 8-10 minutes over medium-high heat.
5. Remove from heat and serve.

NUTRITION FACTS (Per Serving)

Calories: 307, Net Carbs: 12.6 g, Total Carbohydrates: 20.5 g, Total Fat: 8.9 g, Cholesterol 101 mg, Sodium 199 mg, Protein: 37.4 g, Fiber: 7.9 g, Sugar: 6.9 g

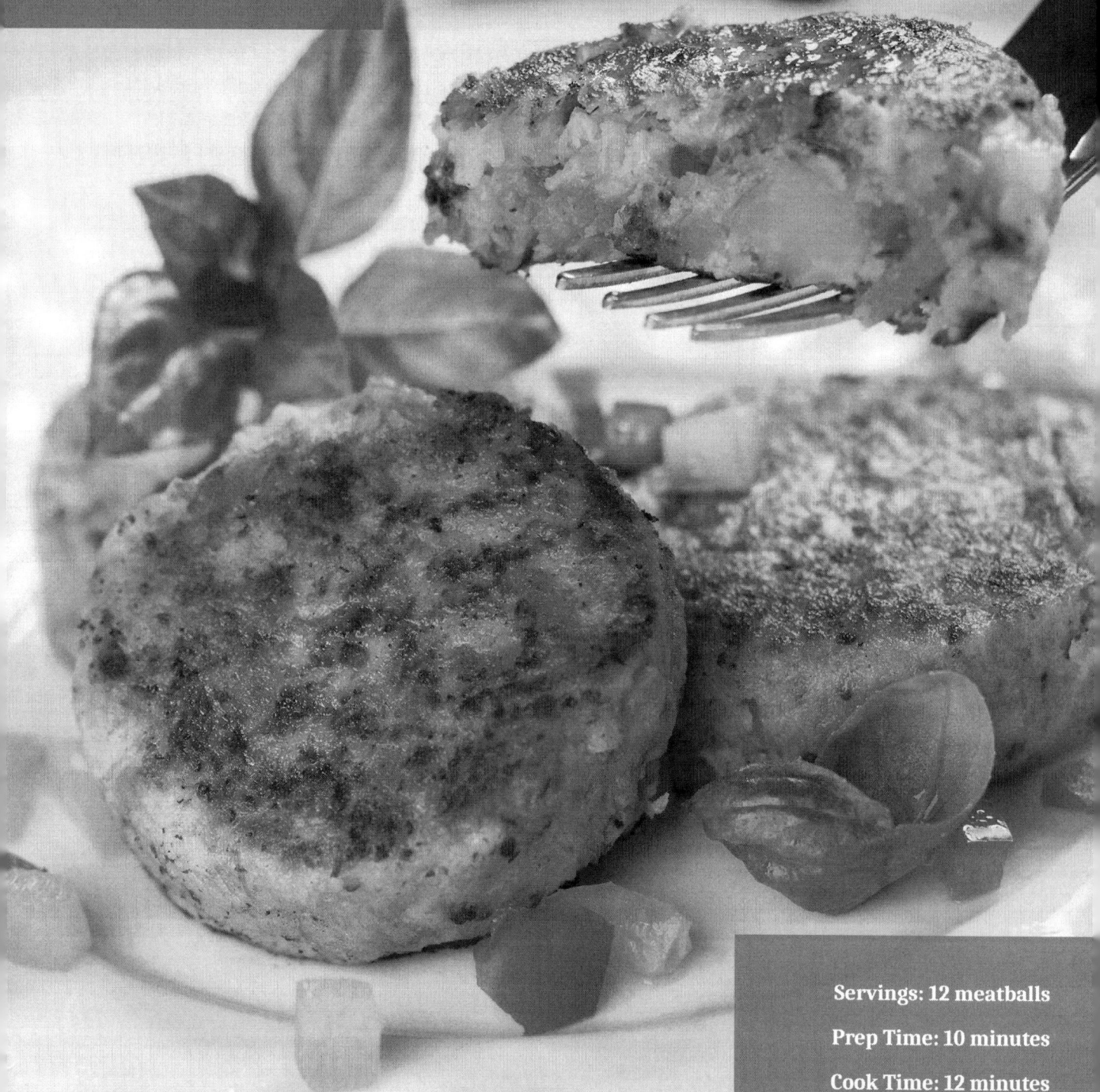

MEAT & POULTRY

Servings: 12 meatballs

Prep Time: 10 minutes

Cook Time: 12 minutes

GREEK TURKEY CUTLETS

Cutlets are a very convenient dish for the weekday family menu. The mixture can be made ahead of time, formed into cutlets, and stored in the freezer. During the week, you can thaw what you need and fry fresh cutlets instead of reheating yesterday's leftovers.

Instead of spinach, you can add broccoli or fresh Mediterranean herbs like rosemary, basil, or oregano.

INGREDIENTS:

- 1 lb. (450 g) ground turkey/chicken
- 1 cup (60 g) fresh spinach, chopped
- 4 oz. (110 g) feta/mozzarella, shredded
- 1 small bell pepper (100 g), finely chopped
- ½ white onion, finely chopped
- 2 garlic cloves, minced
- 1 whole egg, slightly beaten
- ¼ cup (40 g) keto breadcrumbs
- kosher salt
- 4 Tbsp. olive oil, for frying

PROCESS:

1. Thoroughly combine all the ingredients in a bowl.
2. Use your hands to shape small cutlets from the mixture.
3. Preheat olive oil in the skillet.
4. Fry for 8-12 minutes until golden brown, depending on the size of the cutlets. Flip them halfway through.
5. Serve warm with fresh salad.

NUTRITION FACTS (Per Serving)

Calories: 158, Net Carbs: 2.6 g, Total Carbohydrates: 3.5 g, Total Fat: 11.3 g, Cholesterol 60 mg, Sodium 172 mg, Protein: 12.4 g, Fiber: 0.9 g, Sugar: 1.3 g

MEAT & POULTRY

Servings: 3
Prep Time: 10 minutes
Cook Time: 30 minutes

ROASTED PORK TENDERLOIN

You can certainly cook the meat as described in the recipe and get a great flavorful piece of pork. But I recommend searing the pork in hot oil in a pan for 5 minutes on each side before baking. This creates a crispy crust on the outside and juicy meat on the inside. Dijon mustard and aromatic Provencal herbs spice up the meat nicely.

INGREDIENTS:

- 1 lb. (450 g) pork tenderloin
- 3 garlic cloves, minced
- 2 Tbsp. Dijon mustard
- 1 Tbsp. herbs de Provence
- kosher salt

PROCESS:

1. Preheat your oven to 400°F (205°C).

2. Combine all the ingredients, except the tenderloin, in a small bowl.

3. Trim the tenderloin of any excess fat and silverskin. Rub the meat with the mustard mixture and place it in a baking dish.

4. Bake for 20-30 minutes until golden brown, flipping the roast halfway through.

5. Remove from the oven and let the meat rest for 10-15 minutes before serving.

NUTRITION FACTS (Per Serving)

Calories: 228, Net Carbs: 1.1 g, Total Carbohydrates: 1.5 g, Total Fat: 5.8 g, Cholesterol 110 mg, Sodium 205 mg, Protein: 40.4 g, Fiber: 0.4 g, Sugar: 0.1 g

MEAT
& POULTRY

Servings: 4

Prep Time: 10 minutes (plus 2 hours – overnight – marinating time)

Cook Time: 15 minutes

LAMB CHOPS

If you grill the meat, remember to brush it with the leftover marinade from time to time to keep it juicy. Before serving, let the meat stand for 10-15 minutes and brush it with salted herbed butter.

A salad of fresh or grilled vegetables works nicely as an accompaniment.

INGREDIENTS:

- 8 lamb chops 1½ lb. (700 g), patted dry
- herbed salted butter

FOR THE MARINADE:

- 2 Tbsp. grapeseed oil
- 2 Tbsp. Greek yogurt

- 2 garlic cloves, minced
- 1 tsp. dried oregano
- ¼ tsp. lemon pepper
- 1 tsp. fresh lemon juice
- ½ tsp. lemon zest
- ½ tsp. sea salt

PROCESS:

1. Combine all the ingredients for the marinade.

2. Brush lamb chops with the marinade mixture and let rest for 2 hours.

3. Preheat your grill or a frying pan. Cook for 10 minutes for medium-rare and 14 minutes for medium-well. Flip halfway through.

4. Serve with fresh salad or cauliflower rice.

NUTRITION FACTS (Per Serving)

Calories: 412, Net Carbs: 0.4 g, Total Carbohydrates: 0.5 g, Total Fat: 22.1 g, Cholesterol 173 mg, Sodium 176 mg, Protein: 49.8 g, Fiber: 0.1 g, Sugar: 0.3 g

Servings: 4

Prep Time: 8 minutes

Cook Time: 20 minutes

PARMESAN-CRUSTED PORK

The cheese crust adds a tangy flavor to the meat and keeps it juicy. No one likes to eat dry, tough meat. Coating the meat with a crust or cooking it in a sauce prevents just that. You can dip the chops in a beaten egg to make the crust hold up better.

Chops keep well in the refrigerator for several days. They can be reheated in the microwave or oven.

INGREDIENTS:

- 4 pork chops
  (5 oz./140 g each, 1-inch thick), boneless
- ½ cup (60 g) parmesan/cheddar cheese, grated
- 2 garlic cloves, minced

- 2 Tbsp. olive oil
- ¼ tsp. kosher salt
- 1 tsp. onion powder
- 1 tsp. paprika
- ¼ tsp. ground black pepper

PROCESS:

1. Brush pork chops with olive oil.

2. Mix grated cheese with spices, minced garlic, and salt. Cover the pork chops with the cheese mixture.

3. Preheat your oven to 400°F (205°C).

4. Heat olive oil in a skillet. Cook the pork chops for 2 minutes on each side.

5. Transfer them to a baking pan and bake for 13-18 minutes, flipping the pork halfway through.

6. Serve with lemon or lime wedges.

NUTRITION FACTS (Per Serving)

Calories: 562, Net Carbs: 1.6 g, Total Carbohydrates: 1.9 g, Total Fat: 45.1 g, Cholesterol 131 mg, Sodium 238 mg, Protein: 36.8 g, Fiber: 0.3 g, Sugar: 0.3 g

FISH & SEAFOOD

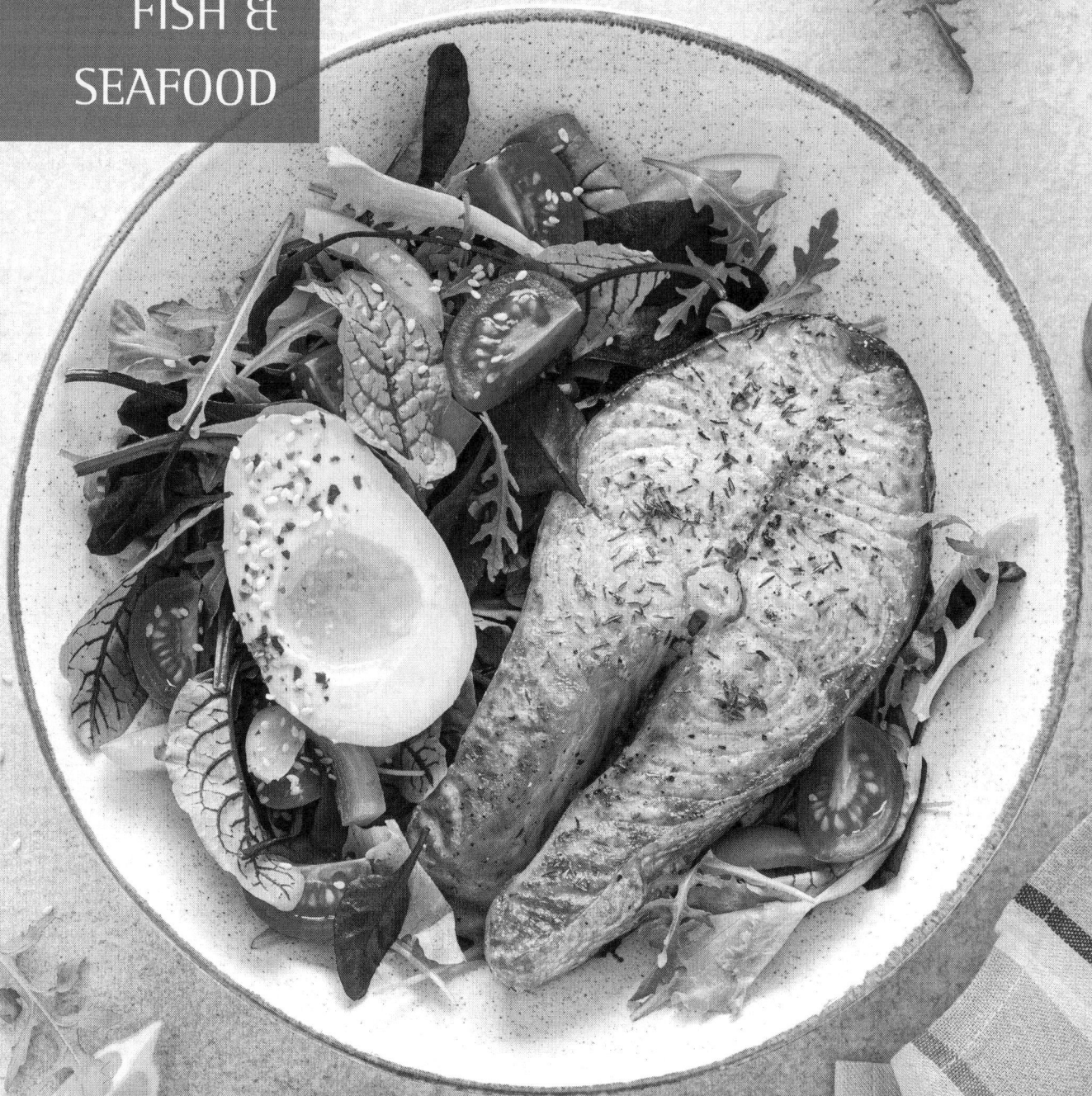

Servings: 4

Prep Time: 20 minutes

Cook Time: 10 minutes

GREEK SALMON WITH FRESH SALAD

Herbs de Provence is a mixture of thyme, rosemary, oregano, basil, and thyme. Of course, you can opt not to use a ready-made mixture but create your own instead, choosing your favorite flavors. You can also add other spices to the marinade, such as paprika, different types of peppers, onion, or garlic powder. The salmon will only benefit from this.

For the salad, choose ingredients with neutral flavors so they don't overpower the delicate flavor of one of the tastiest and healthiest fish.

INGREDIENTS:

- 4 salmon steaks
- olive oil and butter
- lime wedges for sprinkling

FOR THE MARINADE

- 1 Tbsp. extra virgin olive oil
- ½ big lemon, juiced
- 2 garlic cloves, crushed
- 1 Tbsp. herbs de Provence

FOR THE SALAD

- 2 avocados, peeled and halved
- 3 tomatoes (400 g), chopped
- ½ cup fresh arugula
- 2 Tbsp. olive oil
- 1 Tbsp. white wine vinegar
- 1 Tbsp. fresh lemon juice
- ½ cup fresh basil
- ½ cup fresh oregano
- kosher salt

PROCESS:

1. Combine all the ingredients for the marinade and cover the salmon steaks with it. Let the salmon rest in the fridge for 15 minutes.
2. Heat olive oil and butter in a skillet over medium-high heat. Fry salmon steaks for 5 minutes on each side until golden brown.
3. In a serving bowl, combine all the ingredients for the salad.
4. Serve this flaky salmon with the salad and lime wedges.

NUTRITION FACTS (Per Serving)

Calories: 478, Net Carbs: 5 g, Total Carbohydrates: 9.7 g, Total Fat: 35.1 g, Cholesterol 77 mg, Sodium 87 mg, Protein: 36 g, Fiber: 4.7 g, Sugar: 4.4 g

FISH &
SEAFOOD

Servings: 4

Prep Time: 5 minutes

Cook Time: 10 minutes

ROASTED GARLIC SHRIMP

For this recipe, I recommend roasting the shrimp in the oven, but you can also fry them in a pan. I use butter for this. Peeled and unpeeled shrimp of different sizes work great in this recipe, only the cooking time changes. The larger the shrimp, the longer you cook it.

INGREDIENTS:

- 1 lb. (450 g) raw shrimp
- 2 garlic cloves, minced
- ½ tsp. anise seeds
- 1 Tbsp. olive oil
- kosher salt, and lemon pepper

- 2 Tbsp. fresh parsley, finely chopped
- 4 lemon wedges for sprinkling

PROCESS:

1. Preheat your oven to 400°F (205°C).

2. Toss shrimp with minced garlic, anise seeds, olive oil, salt, and pepper.

3. Arrange shrimp on a baking sheet. Roast for 8-10 minutes, depending on the size of the shrimp.

4. Sprinkle with chopped parsley and serve with lemon wedges.

NUTRITION FACTS (Per Serving)

Calories: 170, Net Carbs: 2.8 g, Total Carbohydrates: 3.1 g, Total Fat: 5.1 g, Cholesterol 237 mg, Sodium 276 mg, Protein: 25.9 g, Fiber: .0.3 g, Sugar: 0.2 g

FISH &
SEAFOOD

Servings: 4

Prep Time: 15 minutes

Cook Time: 20 minutes

WHITE FISH CASSEROLE

A casserole is convenient because it is cooked in one dish and does not need anything else to make it a complete meal. The main ingredient of fish is complemented by vegetables. All the ingredients are allowed to steep in the juices and flavors of each other, giving you a delectable, self-sufficient dish.

This casserole is suitable for both a holiday table and a casual family dinner. Choose vegetables for their natural sweetness, preferably in season.

INGREDIENTS:

- 1½ lb. (675 g) white fish fillet (such as halibut or cod)
- kosher salt, black pepper, olive oil
- 1 lemon
- 1 bell pepper (150 g), chopped
- 8 oz. (230 g) halved cherry tomatoes

- 3 oz. (85 g) olives, sliced
- 1 cup (225 g) mozzarella, shredded
- 3 Tbsp. red onion, diced
- 5 garlic cloves, minced
- 2 Tbsp. herbs de Provence

PROCESS:

1. Preheat your oven to 425ºF (220ºC). Brush a baking dish with olive oil.
2. Pat the fish dry with a paper towel. Season all over with salt and pepper.
3. Arrange the fish in the baking dish and sprinkle with the juice of half a lemon.
4. Combine olives, tomatoes, bell peppers, onions, garlic, a pinch of salt and pepper, 3 tablespoons of olive oil, and spices in a bowl and mix well.
5. Pour tomato mixture over the fish. Sprinkle with shredded cheese.
6. Bake for 15-20 minutes. At the 15-minute mark, check if the fish is done by inserting a fork and twisting. If the fish flakes easily, it is done. Remove from the oven and serve.

NUTRITION FACTS (Per Serving)

Calories: 297, Net Carbs: 7 g, Total Carbohydrates: 9.3 g, Protein: 39.5 g, Fat: 11.3 g, Fiber: 2.3 g, Cholesterol 59 mg, Sodium 323 mg, Total Sugars 3.7 g

FISH &
SEAFOOD

Servings: 2

Prep Time: 8 minutes

Cook Time: 25 minutes

WHITE FISH WITH LEMON

Good fresh fish can be prepared in a number of ways, and each offers its own benefits. One way is to steam it for 5 to 6 minutes. The authentic flavor of the fish is fully preserved with this method.

Roasted fish dries out a little in the oven — covering it with vegetables or foil helps to prevent this. For fatty fish, grilling for 3-4 minutes on each side works particularly well.

INGREDIENTS:

- 2 cod/hake/tilapia/haddock fillets (6 oz./170 g each), 1-inch thickness

FOR THE RUB:

- ½ tsp. garlic powder
- ½ tsp. onion powder
- 1 Tbsp. fresh lemon juice
- kosher salt
- olive oil

FOR GARNISH:

- ½ red/yellow/white onion (40 g), cut into strips
- 1 small bell pepper (110 g), wedges
- lettuce
- 4 cherry tomatoes
- 2 Tbsp. olive oil
- salt and pepper to taste

PROCESS:

1. Thoroughly combine all rub ingredients.
2. Lightly drizzle the fish fillets with olive oil. Rub the fish with the garlic-onion mixture.
3. You can grill, roast, or fry the fish, according to your preference.
4. To fry: heat olive oil in a frying pan. Cook for 3-5 minutes on each side.
5. To roast: preheat your oven to 400°F (205°C) and bake the fish for 15-20 minutes.
6. Toss vegetables with olive oil, salt, and pepper.
7. Serve the fish with the vegetable salad drizzled with lime juice.

NUTRITION FACTS (Per Serving)

Calories: 178, Net Carbs: 7.5 g, Total Fat: 1.8 g, Cholesterol 83 mg, Sodium 112 mg, Total Carbohydrate: 9.4 g, Fiber: 1.9 g, Total Sugars 5.5 g, Protein: 31.5 g

FISH &
SEAFOOD

Servings: 6

Prep Time: 15 minutes

Cook Time: 25 minutes

SEAFOOD STEW

This stew is very similar to the famous French ratatouille in its composition of ingredients and cooking method, only with the addition of seafood. All the ingredients complement each other perfectly and serve as an excellent source of micronutrients.

All ingredients require minimal heat treatment to retain their individuality and impart their original flavor in this dish.

INGREDIENTS:

- 8 oz. (230 g) scallops (optional)
- 1½ lb. (675 g) shrimp, peeled and deveined
- 1 zucchini (320 g), chopped
- 1 bell pepper (150 g), chipped
- 1 white onion (70 g), chopped
- 6 garlic cloves, minced
- 3 Tbsp. tomato paste

- 1 Tbsp. dried thyme
- 7 cups (1.7 L) of low-sodium chicken or vegetable broth
- 3 tomatoes, diced
- 1 cup fresh parsley, chopped
- 1 lemon, juiced
- red pepper flakes (optional)
- kosher salt and pepper, to taste
- olive oil

PROCESS:

1. Pat scallops dry and season with sea salt and pepper (if using).

2. Heat 1 tablespoon of olive oil in a frying pan over medium-high heat. Add the scallops, and sear for 2 minutes per side until golden brown. Remove them from the pan and set aside.

3. Add another tablespoon of olive oil to the frying pan and add the shrimp. Cook for 2 minutes. Remove from heat.

4. Heat 1 tablespoon of olive oil in a pot over medium-high heat. Add bell peppers, onions, zucchini, garlic, tomato paste, thyme, and salt. Cook for 5 minutes, stirring occasionally.

5. Pour in the broth and bring it to a boil. Add diced tomatoes and cook for 3-5 minutes. Add lemon juice and parsley. Add scallops and shrimp and continue cooking and stirring for 1-2 minutes. Remove from heat.

NUTRITION FACTS (Per Serving)

Calories: 278, Net Carbs: 12.5 g, Total Fat: 7.4 g, Cholesterol 250 mg, Sodium 444 mg, Total Carbohydrate: 15.4 g, Fiber: 2.9 g, Total Sugars 6.5 g, Protein: 36.5 g

FISH &
SEAFOOD

Servings: 5 cutlets

Prep Time: 10 minutes

Cook Time: 10 minutes

TUNA FISHCAKES

I have made these cutlets from different fish: red fish such as salmon, white fish, and canned fish. Everything works great!

Add chopped bell peppers and onions to the mince if you like juicy cutlets. Also, experiment with additives: try anything from mild Italian herbs to fiery Asian spices.

INGREDIENTS:

- 2 5 oz./140 g cans tuna, drained and shredded
- 1 garlic clove, crushed
- ½ cup (60 g) Parmesan, grated
- 1 cup (150 g) keto breadcrumbs
- ¼ cup (30 g) feta cheese/Mozzarella, crumbled
- 2 whole eggs, slightly beaten

- ½ lemon, juice and zest
- 2 Tbsp. Greek yogurt
- 2 Tbsp. olive oil
- 2 Tbsp. Dijon mustard
- 1 tsp. herbs de Provence/smoked paprika/ thyme
- kosher salt and black pepper
- 2 Tbsp. fresh dill, chopped

PROCESS:

1. Combine all the ingredients in a large bowl and mix well.
2. Shape the tuna mixture into 5 patties using your hands.
3. You can grill them or fry them in a skillet. Cook for 5 minutes on each side until golden brown.
4. Serve warm with grilled or fresh vegetables.

NUTRITION FACTS (Per Serving)

Calories: 230, Net Carbs: 8.4 g, Total Fat: 12.4 g, Cholesterol 88 mg, Sodium 437 mg, Total Carbohydrate: 11.4 g, Fiber: 3 g, Total Sugars .9 g, Protein: 20.3 g

FISH &
SEAFOOD

Servings: 4

Prep Time: 7 minutes

Cook Time: 5 minutes

GOLDEN SCALLOPS

It is a classic combination: scallops with butter, garlic, lemon juice, and fresh Italian herbs. Be sure not to overcook the scallops so they do not become tough and stringy. You want them to remain juicy but with a golden crust on the outside.

Fried scallops pair well with mashed vegetables (broccoli, avocado, cauliflower, etc.), fried asparagus, creamy spinach, roasted Brussels sprouts, or fried zucchini.

INGREDIENTS:

- 1 lb. (450 g) sea scallops
- 2 garlic cloves, minced
- 1 Tbsp. lemon juice
- 2 Tbsp. fresh oregano, chopped
- 2 Tbsp. avocado oil/salted butter, melted
- kosher salt, and pepper
- red pepper flakes

PROCESS:

1. Season scallops with salt and pepper.

2. Heat avocado oil/salted butter in a cast iron skillet or frying pan. Add minced garlic.

3. Arrange scallops in a single layer in the skillet. Cook for 2-3 minutes, depending on the size of the scallops, flipping them once during the cooking process.

4. Add lemon juice, red pepper flakes, chopped oregano, olive oil, salt, and pepper to a small bowl and whisk to combine.

5. Serve scallops with lemon dressing on a bed of mashed broccoli.

NUTRITION FACTS (Per Serving)

Calories: 118, Net Carbs: 3.8 g, Total Fat: 2 g, Cholesterol: 37 mg, Sodium: 183 mg, Total Carbohydrate: 5.1 g, Fiber: 1.3 g, Total Sugars: 0.2 g, Protein: 19.3 g

SOUPS & SAUCES

SOUPS & SAUCES

Servings: 1 cup
Prep Time: 7 minutes
Cook Time: 30 minutes

ITALIAN MARINARA SAUCE

This is a classic Italian tomato sauce with many possible variations. Add white or red onions, olives, capers, and fresh or dried Italian herbs. This version is quick and easy to cook, unlike the typical tomato sauce.

Marinara sauce is used for cooking poultry, meat, seafood, and fish.

INGREDIENTS:

- 1 bay leaf
- black pepper, sea salt
- 7 oz. (200 g) canned crushed tomatoes
- 2 garlic cloves, finely minced
- ¼ Tbsp. olive oil

- 1 Tbsp. fresh basil, chopped
- 1 tsp. red pepper flakes

PROCESS:

1. Add minced garlic, olive oil, and red pepper flakes to a saucepan and place over medium heat. Cook for 2 minutes, stirring continuously.

2. Add the crushed tomatoes, bay leaf, black pepper, chopped basil, and salt.

3. Reduce heat from medium to low and simmer the sauce for 20 minutes, stirring every few minutes. Make sure it doesn't boil too vigorously. It should be bubbling but not splashing your stovetop.

4. Remove from heat, stir, and remove the bay leaf before serving.

NUTRITION FACTS (Per Serving)

Calories: 118, Net Carbs: 3.8 g, Total Fat: 2 g, Cholesterol: 37 mg, Sodium: 183 mg,
Total Carbohydrate: 5.1 g, Fiber: 1.3 g, Total Sugars: 0.2 g, Protein: 19.3 g

Servings: 1 cup

Prep Time: 10 minutes

HOMEMADE PESTO

This bright and herby sauce came to us from Italian Liguria. Traditional recipes call for hard Italian cheeses, such as Parmigiano-Reggiano or Pecorino Sardo, which I have replaced with the more familiar Parmesan.

Also, pine nuts are usually included in this sauce, but they are not a good fit for a keto diet. You can substitute any low-carb nuts: pecans, walnuts, almonds, or macadamia nuts. I recommend roasting them a bit first for a brighter flavor.

INGREDIENTS:

- 2 garlic cloves
- coarse salt, black pepper
- 1 Tbsp. lemon juice
- 3 cups (60 g) fresh basil leaves
- ¼ cup (30 g) pecans, lightly toasted

- ¼ cup (25 g) parmesan, grated
- ¼-½ cup (60-120 ml) extra virgin olive oil

PROCESS:

1. Blend all ingredients in a food processor or high-speed blender.
2. Adjust pepper and salt to taste.
3. Add additional oil if a thinner texture is desired and blend to mix.

NUTRITION FACTS (Per Serving)

Calories: 748, Net Carbs: 4.8 g, Total Fat: 77.7 g, Cholesterol: 18 mg, Sodium: 239 mg, Total Carbohydrate: 9.1 g, Fiber: 4.3 g, Total Sugars: 1.6 g, Protein: 13.3 g

SOUPS & SAUCES

Servings: 4

Prep Time: 10 minutes

SPANISH ROMESCO SAUCE

This tomato-based sauce came to us from Spanish Catalonia. It is a maritime region, so the sauce was initially intended for fish dishes. But over time, it has become so popular that it is also used for cooking poultry and meat.

You can also eat Romesco sauce (or dip) with a slice of bread or wedges of fresh vegetables.

INGREDIENTS:

- 1 big red bell pepper (150 g), roasted and diced
- ¾ cup (100 g) toasted almonds/walnuts/pecans
- ¾ cup (100 g) sun-dried tomatoes
- ¼ cup (60 ml) olive oil
- 4 garlic cloves, roasted in a foil for 15 minutes
- ½ lemon, juiced
- 1 tsp. smoked paprika
- ½ tsp. cayenne pepper
- ½ tsp. kosher salt
- ½ tsp. granulated sweetener

PROCESS:

1. Add all the ingredients to a food processor and blend into a smooth paste.
2. Store in the fridge for 7-8 days or in the freezer for up to 5 months.

NUTRITION FACTS (Per Serving)

Calories: 289, Net Carbs: 6.6 g, Total Fat: 27 g, Cholesterol: 0 mg, Sodium: 3 mg, Total Carbohydrate: 10.8 g, Fiber: 4.2 g, Total Sugars: 4 g, Protein: 6.3 g

SOUPS &
SAUCES

Servings: 8

Prep Time: 15 minutes

Total Time: 12 hours

LEBANESE LABNEH DIP

Try this dip from the Middle East. Labneh is a thick yogurt or soft yogurt cheese. It is easy to make, has a nice thick texture, and is incredibly tasty. Serve it as a dip for vegetables or add it to salads, soups, or pizzas. Also, you can use it as a spread for sandwiches or keto pita bread.

Labneh is healthy not only for its high protein content but also for all the beneficial bacteria that strengthen the immune system.

INGREDIENTS:

- 4 cups (1 L) plain Greek yogurt
- ¼ tsp. kosher salt
- ¼ cup olives, chopped
- 1 tbsp. extra virgin olive oil

- 1 tbsp. fresh parsley, chopped
- 1 tsp. lemon zest
- ¼ tsp. ground sumac

PROCESS:

1. Line a large mesh sieve with four layers of cheesecloth. Place it over a deep bowl leaving at least 3 inches of space between the sieve and the bottom of the bowl.
2. Whisk the yogurt and kosher salt together in a bowl. Transfer the mixture to the cheesecloth.
3. Refrigerate for 12-24 hours.
4. Discard the liquid that has been collected in the bowl.
5. Transfer the thickened yogurt to a serving bowl and drizzle with olive oil. Garnish with chopped olives, parsley, lemon zest, and sumac before serving.

NUTRITION FACTS (Per Serving)

Calories: 30, Net Carbs: 0.9 g, Total Fat: 2.2 g, Cholesterol: 0 mg, Sodium: 44 mg, Total Carbohydrate: 1.1 g, Fiber: 0.2 g, Total Sugars: 0.8 g, Protein: 1.9 g

Servings: 1 cup

Prep Time: 10 minutes

SRIRACHA SAUCE

INGREDIENTS:

- 1 cup (240 ml) plain Greek yogurt
- 2 tbsp. Sriracha
- 1 tsp. smoked paprika
- 2 garlic cloves, peeled
- ¼ tsp. kosher salt
- ¼ tsp. black pepper

PROCESS:

1. Place the garlic in a food processor to dice and blitz it for 2-3 seconds.

2. Add yogurt, paprika, Sriracha, kosher salt, and pepper. Blitz for 2-3 more seconds.

3. Scrape the mixture off the sides of the food processor and blitz for 2 seconds more.

4. Transfer to a bowl and serve.

NUTRITION FACTS (Per Serving)

Calories: 206, Net Carbs: 16.9 g, Total Fat: 3.2 g, Cholesterol: 20 mg, Sodium: 893 mg, Total Carbohydrate: 18.1 g, Fiber: 1.2 g, Total Sugars: 7.8 g, Protein: 23.8 g

SOUPS & SAUCES

Servings: 6

Prep Time: 10 minutes

Cook Time: 20 minutes

SPANISH TOMATO SOUP

The Mediterranean is home to the most delicious tomato soups: the cold Spanish gazpacho, the hearty Salmorejo, or the Italian minestrone. I suggest a versatile tomato cream soup to which you can add a hard-boiled egg, slices of Serrano ham, mozzarella balls, cream cheese, and basil leaves.

This soup is refreshing in summer and warming in winter.

INGREDIENTS:

- 27 oz. (760 ml) canned, whole peeled tomatoes
- 3 Tbsp. dried onion flakes
- 1 cup (30 g) celery, finely chopped
- 2 garlic cloves, minced
- ¼ cup fresh basil leaves

- 2 Tbsp. olive oil
- ½ cup (60 g) pecans
- ½ tsp. kosher salt
- 2 Tbsp. tomato paste
- 2 cups (500 ml) vegetable broth

PROCESS:

1. To a large pot over medium heat, add celery, garlic, olive oil, onion flakes, and salt. Sauté for 7-8 minutes until the celery is softened. Stir in tomato paste.

2. Add the canned tomatoes and bring to a mellow simmer. Allow the soup to simmer uncovered for 10 minutes.

3. Transfer the soup to a food processor or high-speed blender, adding the pecans and basil at the same time. Blend until smooth.

4. Serve with mozzarella balls, boiled eggs, chopped ham, and crispy bread.

NUTRITION FACTS (Per Serving)

Calories: 288, Net Carbs: 7.8 g, Total Carbohydrates: 13 g, Total Fat 25.5 g, Sodium 280 mg, Dietary Fiber: 5.2 g, Total Sugars: 6 g

VEGETABLES

VEGETABLES

Servings: 2

Prep Time: 20 minutes

Cook Time: 60 minutes

STUFFED SPAGHETTI SQUASH

Squash is not a native Mediterranean dish; it was imported from North America. But this winter vegetable has become so beloved and featured in so many recipes that no one doubts it fits the Mediterranean lifestyle.

The most delicious dishes are stuffed pumpkin or zucchini. For stuffing, you can use plant-based ingredients, as in this recipe, or add ground poultry or meat, roasted mushrooms, or sliced olives. Experiment and choose according to your taste.

INGREDIENTS:

- ½ cup baby greens (spinach/arugula), chopped
- 1 cup (250 ml) marinara sauce
- 1 spaghetti squash, halved and seeded
- ½ cup (110 g) ricotta cheese/cream cheese/ mozzarella, crumbled
- crumbled ricotta cheese/feta cheese (for topping)
- sea salt and pepper

PROCESS:

1. Preheat your oven to 350°F (180°C).
2. Spray the cut sides of the squash with olive oil and season with pepper and salt.
3. Place the squash cut side down on a baking sheet and bake for 40-50 minutes or until you can easily pierce the skin with a fork.
4. Remove the baking sheet from the oven and let the squash sit for about 10 minutes.
5. Set the oven to broil.
6. When cool enough to handle, scrape out the squash halves with a fork, taking care not to tear the skins. This will create the spaghetti-like strands that the squash is famous for.
7. In a large bowl, combine the baby greens, marinara sauce, strands of spaghetti squash, and ricotta/ cream cheese/mozzarella.
8. Spoon the squash mixture back into the skins and arrange the squash halves, stuffing side up, on the baking dish.
9. Sprinkle some of the crumbled ricotta over the top of each squash.
10. Broil the stuffed squash for 5-7 minutes until the cheese is golden brown.

NUTRITION FACTS (Per Serving)

Calories: 274, Net Carbs: 10.8 g, Total Carbohydrates: 14 g, Total Fat 10 g, Cholesterol 22 mg, Sodium 635 mg, Dietary Fiber: 3.2 g, Total Sugars: 11 g

VEGETABLES

Servings: 2

Prep Time: 10 minutes

VEGETARIAN SALAD

Artichoke is an entirely Mediterranean plant and has been eaten since the days of ancient Rome and Greece. From there, it spread all over the world. Artichoke is a very valuable source of fiber, vitamins, and minerals.

It resembles asparagus and Brussels sprouts in flavor and properties. It can be eaten raw or cooked, warm or cold, and it fits almost all modern diets.

INGREDIENTS:

- ¼ tsp. crushed red pepper
- ½ tsp. dried rosemary
- ½ tsp. dried thyme
- 2 Tbsp. extra virgin olive oil
- ¼ tsp. garlic powder
- 1 cup (55 g) sun-dried tomatoes, chopped

- 1½ cups marinated artichoke hearts, cut into bite-size pieces
- 1 cup fresh arugula
- ½ cup olives
- kosher salt and pepper
- ½ Tbsp. white wine vinegar

PROCESS:

1. Combine all of the vegetables in a large bowl.

2. In a smaller bowl, combine the garlic powder, olive oil, rosemary, thyme, pepper, salt, and vinegar and briskly whisk until the dressing emulsifies.

3. Coat vegetables with the dressing and serve.

NUTRITION FACTS (Per Serving)

Calories: 355, Net Carbs: 9.1 g, Total Fat: 32.2 g, Cholesterol: 0 mg, Sodium: 628 mg, Total Carbohydrate: 11.1 g, Fiber: 2 g, Total Sugars: 22.8 g, Protein: 1 g

VEGETABLES

Servings: 4

Prep Time: 10 minutes

Cook Time: 25 minutes

FRENCH RATATOUILLE

Ratatouille is a French stew made from vegetables grown in Provence. Like many dishes that are now considered haute cuisine, it was originally a dish eaten by peasants. Similar dishes are found in absolutely every cuisine of the Mediterranean region, and they have all become popular worldwide for their versatility and appealing flavor.

The quality and flavor of each ingredient determine the quality of the finished stew. Therefore, choose only the best organic vegetables, paying attention to the aroma and not the appearance.

INGREDIENTS:

- 1 Tbsp. balsamic vinegar
- 1 bell pepper (150 g), chopped
- black pepper (to taste)
- 1 large eggplant (500 g), chopped
- 3 garlic cloves, minced
- ¼ tsp. ground ginger
- 1 Tbsp. olive oil
- 3 Tbsp. scallions, finely chopped

- ½ tsp. dried thyme
- 1⅓ tsp. smoked paprika
- ¼ tsp. red pepper flakes
- ¼ cup (60 ml) red wine
- ¾ tsp. kosher salt (more to taste)
- fresh thyme, roughly chopped
- 3 tomatoes, chopped
- 1 Tbsp. tomato paste
- 1 large zucchini (400 g), chopped

PROCESS:

1. Heat the oil in a large frying pan over medium heat and sauté the scallions for 4-5 minutes until golden brown.
2. Add chopped eggplant and garlic to the pan and cook for 3-4 minutes. Reduce heat to medium-low.
3. Add ginger, red pepper, oregano, paprika, salt, and wine to the pan and let it simmer for 5-6 minutes, stirring occasionally.
4. Add the bell peppers, tomatoes, and zucchini to the pan and cook until the vegetables are tender.
5. If more liquid is desired, add additional wine.
6. Add the tomato paste and vinegar. Stir to combine. Sample and adjust seasonings to taste.
7. Sprinkle thyme over the stew and serve.

NUTRITION FACTS (Per Serving)

Calories: 125, Net Carbs: 7.3 g, Total Carbohydrates: 14 g, Total Fat 4.5 g, Cholesterol 0 mg, Sodium 22 mg, Dietary Fiber: 6.7 g, Total Sugars: 9.5 g

VEGETABLES

Servings: 4

Prep Time: 10 minutes

Cook Time: 30 minutes

ROASTED VEGETABLES

Almost all Mediterranean herb blends include bay leaf, thyme, and rosemary. They are frequently combined in recipes and can be added to almost all dishes, whether vegetable, fish, or meat.

As a rule, fresh herbs are added at the end of the cooking process or sprinkled over the finished dish. This allows their flavors to shine. On the other hand, dried herbs and spices work better when they are chopped up and added during the cooking process.

INGREDIENTS:

- 1 small eggplant (300 g), diced
- 1 small zucchini (200 g), diced
- 3 Roma tomatoes, diced
- 2 bell peppers (300 g), cut into wedges
- 1 red onion (70 g), quartered
- 4 big garlic cloves, halved
- 1 cup (100 g) button mushrooms, halved

- ½ tsp. red pepper flakes
- 1 tsp. Mediterranean herbs
- ¼ tsp. kosher salt
- 3 Tbsp. olive oil
- 2 Tbsp. lemon juice

PROCESS:

1. Preheat your oven to 400⁰F (205⁰C).
2. Toss vegetables with olive oil, herbs, spices, and salt.
3. Arrange the vegetables in a single layer on a baking sheet.
4. Roast the vegetables for 25-30 minutes, flipping them every 10 minutes.
5. Sprinkle with lemon juice and serve with cubed feta cheese.

NUTRITION FACTS (Per Serving)

Calories: 182, Net Carbs: 13.2 g, Total Fat: 11.2 g, Cholesterol: 0 mg, Sodium: 16 mg,
Total Carbohydrate: 20.4 g, Fiber: 7.2 g, Total Sugars: 11.2 g, Protein: 4.2 g

VEGETABLES

Servings: 4

Prep Time: 10 minutes

Cook Time: 35 minutes

STUFFED BELL PEPPERS

Stuffed peppers are a favorite dish not only for keto diet followers. It combines several popular ingredients: vegetables, meat, and cheese. Moreover, they are quick and almost effortless to prepare. The stuffing can be prepared in advance and stored in the freezer. Simply remove and defrost at the right time, and in 30 minutes, you'll have a fresh, flavorful meal on the table for a family dinner.

INGREDIENTS:

- 4 bell peppers (600 g), wide and short
- 1 lb. (450 g) ground beef/turkey
- 1 cup (200 g) cauliflower rice, cooked
- 1 (15 oz./425 g) can of crushed tomatoes
- 1 small onion (50 g), chopped
- 1 garlic clove, minced
- 1 tsp. dried oregano
- 1 tsp. dried thyme

- ¼ tsp. nutmeg
- ½ tsp. allspice
- ¼ tsp. paprika
- ¼ tsp. sea salt
- ½ Tbsp. olive oil
- 1 cup (120 g) Mozzarella cheese, grated

PROCESS:

FOR THE FILLING:

1. In a large skillet, lightly fry chopped onion and garlic in olive oil until soft.
2. Add ground meat and cook for 5-7 minutes.
3. Remove meat from the heat and add rice, seasonings, ½ cup of grated cheese, crushed tomatoes, and salt.

FOR THE PEPPERS:

4. Preheat your oven to 375°F (190°C).
5. Cut the tops off the peppers and remove everything from the inside. Fill the peppers with stuffing and replace the tops.
6. Arrange peppers on a baking dish, right side up. Bake for 15 minutes. Remove the peppers from the oven and sprinkle ½ cup cheese on top. Return to the oven for another 7-10 minutes.
7. Serve warm garnished with fresh basil.

NUTRITION FACTS (Per Serving)

Calories: 329, Net Carbs: 13 g, Total Carbohydrates: 17 g, Sodium 157 mg, Fat: 11 g, Protein: 39 g, Fiber: 4 g, Sugar: 11 g

VEGETABLES

Servings: 4

Prep Time: 7 minutes

Cook Time: 15 minutes

ROASTED ASPARAGUS

The season of crisp and juicy asparagus is so short we should enjoy it to the fullest. I want to eat it minimally cooked, without additives or spices, so I can remember its fleeting flavor all year long until the following spring.

I recommend roasted asparagus with a light tahini sauce that doesn't overshadow its flavor and crunchy texture.

INGREDIENTS:

- 1 lb. (450 g) fresh asparagus
- 1 Tbsp. sesame seeds/feta cheese
- 1 Tbsp. olive oil
- kosher salt, and black pepper

FOR THE TAHINI SAUCE:

- 3 Tbsp. tahini
- 1 lemon, zest, and juice
- 1 garlic clove, crushed
- 2 Tbsp. water
- 2 Tbsp. sesame oil
- ½ tsp. sea salt
- ¼ tsp. paprika

PROCESS:

1. Cut off the hard, woody ends of the asparagus and peel away any tough parts. Sprinkle with olive oil, salt, and pepper.

2. Preheat your oven to 400°F (205°C). Arrange asparagus in a single layer on the baking sheet. Bake for 8-15 minutes until it is crisp-tender.

3. Blend all ingredients for the tahini sauce.

4. Drizzle asparagus with tahini sauce and sprinkle with sesame seeds.

NUTRITION FACTS (Per Serving)

Calories: 198, Net Carbs: 4.8 g, Total Fat: 17.7 g, Cholesterol: 0 mg, Sodium: 16 mg, Total Carbohydrate: 9 g, Fiber: 4.2 g, Total Sugars: 2.6 g, Protein: 5 g

VEGETABLES

Servings: 4

Prep Time: 10 minutes

Cook Time: 15 minutes

ZUCCHINI SALAD

INGREDIENTS:

- 1 lb. (450 g)/2 medium zucchini, diced
- sea salt, and pepper
- ½ tsp. cumin
- 2 Tbsp. olive oil, divided
- ½ lemon, juiced
- 2 garlic cloves, minced

- ½ cup (30 g) fresh dill, chopped
- 1 Tbsp. fresh basil, chopped
- ½ cup (60 g) feta cheese, crumbled

PROCESS:

1. Preheat your oven to 425⁰F (220⁰C).

2. Toss zucchini with salt, pepper, cumin, and 1 tablespoon olive oil.

3. Arrange zucchini in a single layer on a baking sheet. Cook for 10-15 minutes, flipping halfway through.

4. Combine roasted zucchini, lemon juice, garlic, and chopped herbs in a bowl.

5. Sprinkle with crumbled feta cheese.

NUTRITION FACTS (Per Serving)

Calories: 149, Net Carbs: 6.8 g, Total Carbohydrates: 8.8 g, Fat: 11 g, Protein: 5 g, Sodium 236 mg, Fiber: 2 g, Sugar: 3 g

VEGETABLES

Servings: 4

Prep Time: 10 minutes

Cook Time: 20 minutes

CRISPY CABBAGE

This versatile recipe works for any type of cabbage. You can use Brussels sprouts, red cabbage, or even cauliflower in place of white cabbage. Roast at high temperature so the cabbage will crisp up but still be juicy. Take care not to let it dry out.

Roasted cabbage is a good side dish for chicken or bacon.

INGREDIENTS:

- 1 head green/red cabbage (800 g), cut into wedges/steaks
- avocado oil spray
- kosher salt
- 1 tsp. onion powder
- 1 tsp. garlic powder

FOR THE TAHINI SAUCE:

- 3 Tbsp. tahini
- 1 lemon (90 g), zest, and juice
- 1 garlic clove, crushed
- 2 Tbsp. water
- 2 Tbsp. sesame oil
- ½ tsp. kosher salt
- ¼ tsp. paprika
- 2 Tbsp. green onion, chopped

PROCESS:

1. Spray cabbage wedges with avocado oil and season with sea salt, garlic powder, and onion powder.

2. Preheat your oven to 400°F (205°C). Arrange cabbage wedges in a single layer on a baking dish. Bake for 20 minutes, flipping halfway through.

3. Combine all ingredients for the tahini sauce.

4. Serve roasted cabbage with tahini sauce.

NUTRITION FACTS (Per Serving)

Calories: 193, Net Carbs: 10.2 g, Total Fat: 13.7 g, Cholesterol: 0 mg, Sodium: 51 mg, Total Carbohydrate: 17.1 g, Fiber: 6.9 g, Total Sugars: 7.3 g, Protein: 5 g

VEGETABLES

Servings: 4

Prep Time: 5 minutes

Cook Time: 50 minutes

FABULOUS ROASTED TOMATOES

Roasted tomatoes are the most recognizable Mediterranean dish. They start every cookbook and always appear in dining scenes when the director wants to transport the movie viewer to Tuscany or Provence. They make our mouths water and inspire us to turn the pages further.

The secret to preparing this dish is undeniably simple: choose the right seasonal tomatoes, focusing on their aroma. Baking only accentuates the sour-sweet flavor — it can't correct it if the tomatoes are of poor quality to begin with.

INGREDIENTS:

- 4-5 ripe small tomatoes, halved
- olive oil/avocado oil spray
- 6 garlic cloves, finely chopped
- ½ tsp. red pepper flakes
- ¼ tsp. sea salt
- a bunch of fresh thyme, basil, oregano, chopped

PROCESS:

1. Spray tomato halves with avocado oil and season with salt and red pepper.
2. Preheat your oven to 320°F (160°C). Arrange the tomatoes in a single layer on the baking sheet. Bake for 40-50 minutes.
3. Sprinkle the tomato halves with chopped garlic and herbs. Cook for 5 minutes more.
4. Serve warm with crispy keto bread.

NUTRITION FACTS (Per Serving)

Calories: 64, Net Carbs: 5.3 g, Total Fat: 3.7 g, Cholesterol: 0 mg, Sodium: 8 mg, Total Carbohydrate: 7.6 g, Fiber: 2.3 g, Total Sugars: 3.3 g, Protein: 1.6 g

DESSERTS

Servings: 12 tarts

Prep Time: 40 minutes

Cook Time: 25 minutes

BERRY TARTLETS

INGREDIENTS:

PASTRY:

- 1¼ cup (140 g) almond flour
- 3 Tbsp. (45 g) powdered monk fruit sweetener/sub with powdered erythritol
- 1 tsp keto baking powder
- ¼ tsp kosher salt
- ¼ tsp xanthan gum
- 1 large egg, whisked
- 2 Tbsp. (30 g) unsalted butter, melted

FILLING:

- ¼ cup (60 g) unsalted butter
- ⅓ cup (75 g) golden monk fruit sweetener/ sub with erythritol
- ⅓ cup (75 g) allulose/sub with erythritol
- ½ cup (120 g) heavy cream
- ½ tsp caramel extract/sub with vanilla extract
- ¼ tsp xanthan gum
- ⅛ tsp kosher salt
- 1 large egg, whisked
- 2 Tbsp. dried currants

NUTRITION FACTS (Per Serving)

Calories 165, Net Carbs: 3 g, Total Fat 13.7 g, Total Carbohydrates 4.2 g, Dietary Fiber 1.2 g, Protein 3.3 g

PROCESS:

PASTRY:

1. Preheat the oven to 325°F (163°C) and lightly grease a muffin tin with coconut oil.

2. Add the almond flour, powdered monk fruit, baking powder, and salt to a large bowl. Whisk to combine the dry ingredients and remove any hard clumps.

3. Add the beaten egg and melted butter and stir until a dough forms. Shape the dough into a ball.

4. Transfer the dough to a work surface that you have lightly dusted with almond flour. Cover the dough with parchment paper and roll it out until it is ⅛-inch thick.

5. Use a 3½-inch cookie cutter (or the mouth of a drinking glass) to cut out the tart crusts.

6. Use a spatula to carefully transfer the tart crusts to the prepared muffin tin.

7. Gently press the dough into the muffin cup.

8. Continue to reroll the pastry and cut out circles until the dough is used up. You should have 12 pastry circles.

9. Place the muffin tin in the freezer and begin to prepare the filling.

FILLING:

10. Add the butter and golden monk fruit to a medium-sized saucepan and warm over medium heat.

11. When the mixture is hot, remove the pan from the heat and pour in the heavy cream and vanilla extract. The hot mixture will bubble and spurt.

12. Add the xanthan gum to the saucepan and whisk thoroughly to ensure it is fully incorporated.

13. Next, whisk in the salt.

14. Set aside and allow to cool for approximately 10 minutes.

15. While the filling is cooling, remove the tart shells from the freezer.

16. Return to the cooled filling and add the whisked egg. Stir to combine thoroughly.

17. Spoon the filling into each tart shell, filling the crust almost to the top.

18. Bake for 18-22 minutes until the edges are golden and the center retains a slight jiggle.

19. Allow the tarts to cool completely in the muffin tin, and then use a knife to loosen and remove each tart carefully. Decorate with fresh berries.

DESSERTS

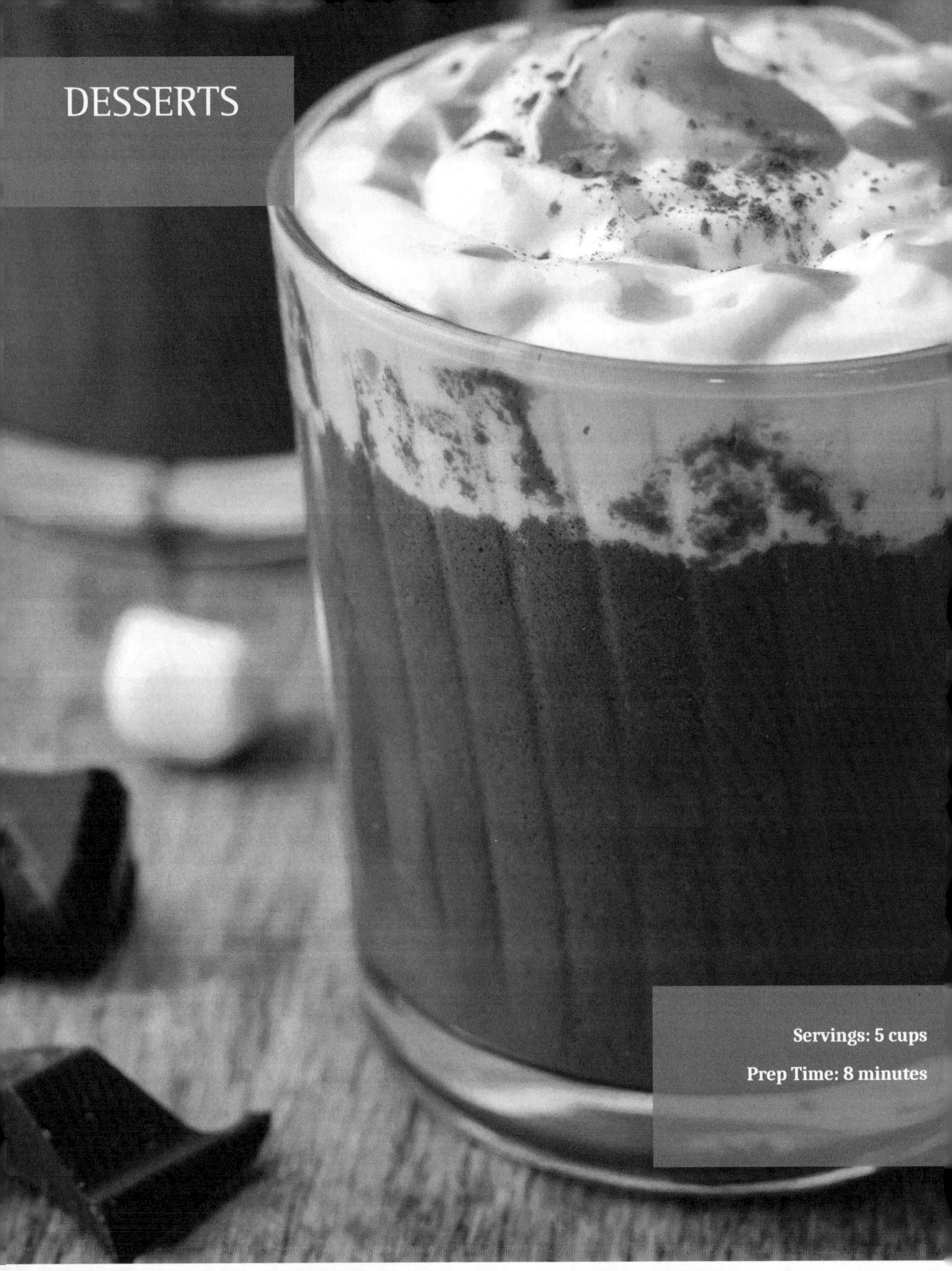

Servings: 5 cups

Prep Time: 8 minutes

CHOCOLATE COCONUT MOUSSE

Chocolate mousse is the most famous French dessert. To adapt it to the keto diet, we had to change it so much that only the name remains from the original. But I hope our chocolate keto mousse will please you to a degree worthy of the finest French desserts.

INGREDIENTS:

- 13.5 oz. (380 ml) can full-fat coconut milk
- ¼ cup stevia
- ⅓ cup (30 g) unsweetened cocoa powder

OPTIONAL ADDITIONS:
- ½ tsp. vanilla extract
- ¼ tsp. instant coffee

PROCESS:

1. Chill a large mixing bowl.

2. Chill the coconut milk (and vanilla extract, if using).

3. Open the can of coconut milk and drain off the water. Pour only the thick crème remaining into the chilled bowl.

4. Using an electric mixer set on high, whip the coconut crème until stiff peaks form.

5. Add the rest of the ingredients and whip until a smooth texture is achieved.

6. Serve with unsweetened whipped cream.

NUTRITION FACTS (Per Serving)

Calories: 97, Net Carbs: 2 g, Total Fat: 9.2 g, Cholesterol: 0 mg, Sodium: 9 mg, Total Carbohydrate: 4 g, Fiber: 2 g, Total Sugars: 0.1 g, Protein: 1.9 g

DESSERTS

Servings: 8 biscotti

Prep Time: 15 minutes

Cook Time: 1 hour

ITALIAN BISCOTTI

Chocolate mousse is the most famous French dessert. To adapt it to the keto diet, we had to change it so much that only the name remains from the original. But I hope our chocolate keto mousse will please you to a degree worthy of the finest French desserts.

INGREDIENTS:

- 1½ cups (170 g) almond flour
- 2 Tbsp. arrowroot flour
- 2 large eggs
- ½ cup (70 g) whole almonds
- ½ cup (60 g) dried cranberries/chocolate chips/macadamia nuts
- ⅓ cup (70 g) granular Swerve sweetener
- One lemon, zested
- 1 tsp. vanilla
- ¼ tsp. sea salt
- ½ tsp. baking soda

PROCESS:

1. Preheat your oven to 350°F (180°C) and line a baking sheet with parchment paper.
2. Combine lemon zest, vanilla, sweetener, and eggs in a bowl. Use an electric mixer to beat until frothy.
3. Add flour, salt, and baking soda, and mix until a dough forms. Add almonds and cranberries and stir to incorporate thoroughly.
4. Spread the dough in a long rectangle on the prepared baking sheet. Bake for 20 minutes until golden brown.
5. Remove from the oven and let it cool for 30 minutes. After it has cooled significantly, cut the dough into long strips at a slight angle.
6. Arrange the cut slices in a single layer on the baking sheet and place them in the oven for another 15-20 minutes. This will give them that extra crunch.
7. Allow the biscotti to cool completely before serving.

NUTRITION FACTS (Per Serving)

Calories: 162, Net Carbs: 12.3 g, Total Fat: 12.2 g, Cholesterol: 47 mg, Sodium: 161 mg,
Total Carbohydrate: 15.4 g, Fiber: 3.1 g, Total Sugars: 9.7 g, Protein: 6.6 g

DESSERTS

Servings: 6

Prep Time: 5 minutes

Cook Time: 2 hours

CHOCOLATE BONBONS

INGREDIENTS:

- 5 Tbsp. (70 g) softened butter
- 3 Tbsp. coconut oil
- 2 Tbsp. sugar-free raspberry syrup/ 1 tsp. vanilla extract/ ½ tsp. almond extract
- 2 Tbsp. cocoa powder
- 1 tsp. keto sweetener (optional)

FOR COATING (optional)
- coconut chips
- cocoa powder
- sesame seeds

PROCESS:

1. Combine all the ingredients in a bowl and mix well.
2. Divide the mixture evenly between six molds or muffin tins.
3. Place the filled molds in the freezer for a minimum of two hours until they are firmly set.

NUTRITION FACTS (Per Serving)

Net Carbs 5.6 g, Calories 163, Total Fat 14.6 g, Saturated Fat 7.6 g, Cholesterol 0 mg, Sodium 2 mg, Total Carbohydrate 7.6 g, Dietary Fiber 2 g, Total Sugars 4.5 g, Protein 3.3 g, Calcium 9 mg, Iron 3 mg, Potassium 144 mg

DESSERTS

Servings: 20 – 24 cookies

Prep Time: 20 minutes

Cook Time: 20 minutes

SPANISH ALMOND COOKIES

INGREDIENTS:

- 1½ cups (170 g) almond flour
- ½ cup (100 g) erythritol
- 24 almonds (25 g)
- 1 whole egg, beaten
- 1 tsp. lemon extract
- 1 Tbsp. lemon zest

PROCESS:

1. Preheat your oven to 350°F (180°C) and line a baking sheet with parchment paper.

2. Combine beaten eggs, zest, flour, lemon extract, and erythritol. Mix with your hand until a smooth dough forms.

3. Using a tablespoon to measure the dough, form each cookie into an oval shape and arrange them on the baking sheet. You should have 24 cookies. Take care to make them all uniform in size and shape.

4. Firmly press an almond into the top of each cookie.

5. Bake the cookies for 20 minutes and let them cool completely before serving.

6. These cookies can be stored in an airtight container for up to one week, but I do not recommend freezing them.

NUTRITION FACTS (Per Serving)

Calories: 38, Net Carbs: 4.7 g, Total Fat: 292 g, Cholesterol: 7 mg, Sodium: 4 mg, Total Carbohydrate: 5.4 g, Fiber: 0.7 g, Total Sugars: 4.3 g, Protein: 1.6 g

BAKING

Servings: 8 slices

Prep Time: 40 minutes

Cook Time: 30 minutes

BRETON MUSHROOM GALETTE

INGREDIENTS:

PASTRY DOUGH:

- ¾ cup (90 g) almond flour
- ½ cup (55 g) coconut flour
- 1 tsp. keto baking powder
- 1½ tsp. salt
- ¾ cup (180 g) unsalted butter
- 2 large eggs, whisked
- 1½ cups (330 g) mozzarella cheese, shredded

MUSHROOM AND ONION FILLING:

- ¼ cup (60 g) unsalted butter
- 2 Tbsp. olive oil
- 1 lb. (450 g) sliced mushrooms (Portobello/ shiitake)
- ½ cup yellow onion, chopped
- 2 garlic cloves, minced
- kosher salt and pepper, to taste
- 4 oz. (110 g) goat cheese

NUTRITION FACTS (Per Serving)

Calories: 396, Net Carbs: 5.9 g, Total Fat: 34.5 g, Cholesterol: 116 mg, Sodium: 272 mg, Total Carbohydrate: 10.4 g, Fiber: 4.5 g, Total Sugars: 1.7 g, Protein: 13.6 g

PROCESS:

PASTRY DOUGH:

1. Combine the coconut and almond flours, baking powder, and salt in a medium-sized bowl and whisk together.

2. In a small saucepan over medium heat, melt the butter.

3. Add the melted butter to the dry ingredients and incorporate it quickly.

4. Next, add beaten eggs and combine thoroughly.

5. Heat the mozzarella cheese in the microwave for 90 seconds or until melted. Stir the cheese at the halfway point.

6. Add the melted cheese to the mixture and use your hands to knead it into a stiff dough. Ensure all the ingredients are fully incorporated. The dough will be sticky. Try sandwiching the dough between two sheets of parchment paper to make kneading easier.

7. Cover the dough and refrigerate for 20 minutes.

FILLING:

8. Heat the butter and olive oil in a large frying pan over medium heat.

9. Add the mushrooms and onions and sauté until the onions are translucent.

10. Add the minced garlic, salt, and pepper, and heat through for 1 minute, stirring constantly.

ASSEMBLE:

11. Preheat the oven to 375°F (190°C) and set aside a large baking tray.

12. Remove the chilled dough from the fridge and work it by folding it onto itself several times. This encourages flaky layers of pastry.

13. On a large piece of parchment paper, roll out the dough into a circle approximately 14 inches in diameter.

14. Sprinkle an even layer of goat cheese over the dough, leaving a 2-inch border along the edges.

15. Next, spread an even layer of mushroom and onion filling.

16. Fold the 2-inch border of dough up and over the edges of the filling. If any cracks appear, press the dough back together.

17. Once the edges are folded, use your hands to gently mold the galette and reinforce its circular shape.

18. Use the parchment paper to carefully transfer the galette to the baking sheet. Bake for 25–30 minutes until the crust is golden.

19. Leftovers can be refrigerated in an airtight container for up to 3 days.

BAKING

Servings: 10

Prep Time: 15 minutes

Cook Time: 25 minutes

ITALIAN FOCACCIA

INGREDIENTS:

- 3 cups (340 g) almond flour
- ½ cup (120 ml) almond milk
- 5 large whole eggs, separated
- 10-2 cherry tomatoes/sun-dried tomatoes
- ½ cup (20 g) basil leaves/olives
- 1 Tbsp. extra virgin olive oil

- 1 tsp. apple cider vinegar
- 1 tsp. fine sea salt
- 2 tsp. baking powder
- 1 tsp. coarse sea salt, for sprinkling

PROCESS:

1. Line a 9x13-inch baking sheet with parchment paper and preheat the oven to 350°F (180°C).

2. Combine salt, baking powder, and almond flour in a large bowl and mix until well combined.

3. Beat one egg and add it to the flour mixture along with the almond milk and apple cider vinegar. Mix well until a smooth dough forms. Set aside to rest.

4. Separate the whites from the yolks in the four remaining eggs. With an electric mixer, beat the egg whites until stiff peaks form.

5. Add egg whites to the flour mixture and fold in gently, taking care not to deflate the whites.

6. Gently spoon the dough onto the prepared baking sheet. Top with cherry tomatoes, basil leaves, and coarse salt, and drizzle with extra-virgin olive oil.

7. Bake for 20-25 minutes until lightly golden. Allow to cool completely before removing it from the baking sheet and serving.

8. This will keep in the refrigerator for up to 5 days in an airtight container.

NUTRITION FACTS (Per Serving)

Calories: 220, Net Carbs: 3.5 g, Total Fat: 17.5 g, Cholesterol: 93 mg, Sodium: 48 mg, Total Carbohydrate: 7.7 g, Fiber: 3.2 g, Total Sugars: 1.6 g, Protein: 8.6 g

BAKING

Servings: 8 baguettes

Prep Time: 15 minutes

Cook Time: 30-45 minutes

FRENCH BAGUETTE

INGREDIENTS:

- 1½ cups (150 g) almond flour
- ½ cup (60 g) coconut flour
- ½ cup (750 g) flax meal
- ⅓ cup (40 g) psyllium husk powder
- 6 egg whites
- 2 large whole eggs

- ¾ cup (180 ml) buttermilk
- 1 cup (240 ml) lukewarm water
- ¼ cup (60 ml) white wine vinegar
- 1 tsp. sea salt
- 1 tsp. baking soda

PROCESS:

1. Line a baking sheet with parchment paper and preheat the oven to 400°F (205°C).

2. Mix almond flour, coconut flour, psyllium husk, flax meal, baking soda, and salt in a large bowl. Set aside.

3. Combine buttermilk, two whole eggs, and the egg whites in another bowl. Add this mixture to the dry ingredients and mix until a smooth dough forms.

4. Add the white wine vinegar and water and mix until just combined.

5. Form eight baguettes from the dough and place them on the prepared baking sheet. Leave space between them to allow them to rise and expand.

6. Bake for 10 minutes at the set temperature, then reduce the temperature to 340°F (170°C) and continue to bake for another 30 minutes.

7. Allow baguettes to cool completely on the baking sheet before serving. Refrigerate for up to 1 week or freeze for up to 3 months.

NUTRITION FACTS (Per Serving)

Calories: 598, Net Carbs: 5.5 g, Total Fat: 44.5 g, Cholesterol: 47 mg, Sodium: 230 mg,
Total Carbohydrate: 42.7 g, Fiber: 37.2 g, Total Sugars: 1.4 g, Protein: 30.6 g

BAKING

Servings: 8 baguettes

Prep Time: 15 minutes

Cook Time: 30-45 minutes

GARLIC GRISSINI

It's hard to imagine even one Italian restaurant without these breadsticks. Not surprisingly, there are an almost infinite number of variations. I love these cheese sticks with coconut flour. They can be rolled in cheese, sesame seeds, or wrapped in bacon.

INGREDIENTS:

- ⅔ cup (85 g) coconut flour
- 3 cups (340 g) shredded mozzarella cheese
- 4 whole eggs
- 4 Tbsp. cream cheese
- 1 Tbsp. butter, melted
- 1 tsp. garlic powder

- 1 tsp. oregano
- 1 tsp. sea salt
- 1 tsp. baking powder
- 1 cup (240 ml) of water to add as needed

PROCESS:

1. Line a baking sheet with parchment paper and preheat your oven to 350ºF (180ºC).

2. Melt the shredded mozzarella cheese with the cream cheese in the microwave. Stir to combine.

3. Add garlic powder, eggs, flour, oregano, and salt. Mix again to form a stiff dough. If the dough is too dry and not coming together easily, add one tablespoon of water at a time until the dough holds together.

4. Using oiled hands, divide the dough into eight portions and shape it into breadsticks. Arrange them on the baking sheet.

5. Brush the breadsticks with melted butter and bake them in the preheated oven for 20 minutes. When done, the breadsticks should be firm to the touch and lightly golden brown.

6. Serve with meat, olives, and cheese.

NUTRITION FACTS (Per Serving)

Calories: 191, Net Carbs: 5.8 g, Total Fat: 11.5 g, Cholesterol: 130 mg, Sodium: 172 mg, Total Carbohydrate: 12 g, Fiber: 6.2 g, Total Sugars: 0.4 g, Protein: 10.6 g

BAKING

VEGETABLE QUICHE

INGREDIENTS:

- pre-made keto almond pie crust
- 1 cup (113 g) cheddar cheese, shredded
- 1 red onion (70 g), diced
- 2 garlic cloves, minced
- 1 red bell pepper (130 g), diced
- 2 cups (60 g) broccoli florets
- ⅓ cup (40 g) feta cheese, crumbled
- 4 whole eggs
- 1¼ cups (300 ml) whole milk
- 1 tsp. dried oregano
- 1 tsp. dried parsley
- 2 tbsp. salted butter
- kosher salt, and pepper, to taste

PROCESS:

1. Preheat your oven to 375°F (190°C). Place the crust on a pie plate and flute the edges.

2. Melt the butter in a skillet over medium-high heat. Add garlic and onion and cook for 3 minutes, constantly stirring, until the onions are tender. Add red pepper and cook for 3 more minutes, occasionally stirring, until the pepper is tender.

3. Add broccoli, parsley, and oregano, and cook for 5 more minutes, stirring occasionally.

4. Remove from heat. Add the feta cheese and mix well.

5. Transfer the mixture to the pie crust and spread evenly.

6. Whisk together eggs, milk, sea salt, pepper, and ½ cup cheese. Pour the egg mixture over the vegetables at the bottom of the crust. Sprinkle the rest of the cheddar cheese over the top.

7. Bake for 50-55 minutes. It is done when the crust is golden brown, and the eggs have set.

8. Remove the quiche from the oven and let it cool for 10-15 minutes before serving.

NUTRITION FACTS (Per Serving)

Calories: 191, Net Carbs: 5.2 g, Total Fat: 12.5 g, Cholesterol: 113 mg, Sodium: 230 mg, Total Carbohydrate: 8.8 g, Fiber: 3.6 g, Total Sugars: 3.9 g, Protein: 11.3 g

BAKING

Servings: 2 buns

Prep Time: 1 hour 50 minutesCook

Time: 40 minutes

KETO CIABATTA

INGREDIENTS:

- 1 cup (110 g) superfine almond flour
- 1 cup vital wheat gluten
- ¼ cup (40 g) flaxseed meal
- ½ cup + 2 Tbsp. (140 ml) lukewarm water
- 1 Tbsp. unsalted butter, melted
- 3 Tbsp. olive oil

- 1 tsp. sugar
- ¾ tsp. kosher salt
- 2¼ tsp. active dry yeast
- 1½ tsp. keto baking powder

PROCESS:

1. Line a baking sheet with parchment paper.

2. Mix ½-cup warm water, sugar, and yeast in a medium-sized bowl. Cover the bowl and allow it to sit until bubbles rise to the surface and the mixture appears foamy.

3. In a large bowl, combine almond flour, wheat gluten, flaxseed meal, salt, and baking powder.

4. Add olive oil and remaining water to the yeast mixture, then add this to the dry ingredients. Mix well to form a wet dough.

5. Knead this dough for about 4 minutes, but don't overmix.

6. Divide the dough and shape it into two short cylinders of roughly 2½x7 inches. Transfer them to the prepared baking sheet.

7. Preheat your oven to 110°F (45°C) and turn it off. Place the dough in the warm oven and leave it to rise for up to one hour. After they have risen, remove the loaves from the oven and set the temperature to 350°F (180°C).

8. Brush the loaves with the melted butter and bake them in the preheated oven for 40 minutes. Brush the loaves with butter every 10 to 15 minutes as they bake.

9. When done, remove the loaves from the oven and allow them to cool completely on the baking sheet before serving.

NUTRITION FACTS (Per Serving)

Calories: 191, Net Carbs: 5.2 g, Total Fat: 12.5 g, Cholesterol: 113 mg, Sodium: 230 mg, Total Carbohydrate: 8.8 g, Fiber: 3.6 g, Total Sugars: 3.9 g, Protein: 11.3 g

Servings: 12 slices

Prep Time: 20 minutes

Cook Time: 60 minutes

ITALIAN OLIVE BREAD

INGREDIENTS:

- 1½ cups (170 g) almond flour
- 5 Tbsp. ground flaxseed
- 2 Tbsp. psyllium husk powder
- ½ cup (120 ml) sour cream
- 4 large eggs
- ½ cup (120 ml) olive oil

- 1.7 oz. (50 g) olives, chopped
- 2 Tbsp. apple cider vinegar
- 1 tsp. dried oregano
- 1 tsp. dried basil
- 1 tsp. sea salt
- 1 tsp. baking soda

PROCESS:

1. Combine almond flour, baking soda, flaxseed, oregano, psyllium husk powder, and salt, and set aside.

2. Using an electric mixer, beat the eggs in a separate bowl for 3 minutes until frothy and light. Gradually add olive oil to the mixture, creating a smooth emulsion. Then add sour cream and apple cider vinegar, continuing to beat until completely combined.

3. Gradually add the dry ingredients to the wet ingredients. As the dough becomes stiffer and more difficult to work with, switch to the dough hook on your stand mixer or your hands if using an electric beater.

4. Finally, add the chopped olives to the dough and mix to distribute evenly. Cover the dough and let it rest for 15 minutes at room temperature.

5. In the meantime, preheat your oven to 390°F (200°C) and grease a bread pan with olive oil or coconut oil.

6. Transfer the dough to the bread pan and bake for 30 minutes. Then reduce the temperature to 300°F (150°C) and bake for another 30 minutes.

7. Serve with cheese, tomatoes, or soup.

NUTRITION FACTS (Per Serving)

Calories: 205, Net Carbs: 1.8 g, Total Fat: 18.5 g, Cholesterol: 66 mg, Sodium: 172 mg, Total Carbohydrate: 4.9 g, Fiber: 3.1 g, Total Sugars: 0.2 g, Protein: 5 g

Servings: 8

Prep Time: 10 minutes

Cook Time: 15 minutes

CHEESY GARLIC BREAD

INGREDIENTS:

- ½ cup (120 g) unsalted butter, softened
- ¼ cup (60 ml) mayonnaise
- 1 tsp. garlic powder
- 1 tsp. onion powder
- 2 cups (230 g) shredded mozzarella cheese
- ½ cup (90 g) olives, chopped
- 1 loaf of keto French Bread, halved lengthwise

PROCESS:

1. Preheat the oven to 350°F (177°F).
2. Stir butter and mayonnaise together until smooth and creamy.
3. Add onion powder, garlic powder, olives, and cheese and stir to combine.
4. Spread the mixture over the French bread.
5. Place the bread on a baking sheet and bake for 10-12 minutes.
6. Finish by placing the bread under the broiler until the cheese has melted and the bread is golden brown.

NUTRITION FACTS (Per Serving)

Calories: 308, Net Carbs: 9.5 g, Total Fat: 17.8 g, Saturated Fat: 9.1 g, Cholesterol: 37 mg, Sodium: 479 mg, Total Carbohydrate: 11.1 g, Dietary Fiber: 1.6 g, Total Sugars: 2 g, Protein: 7.8 g, Vitamin D: 0 mcg, Calcium: 42 mg, Iron: 2 mg, Potassium: 75 mg

BAKING

Servings: 10 slices

Prep Time: 15 minutes

Cook Time: 50 minutes

ITALIAN HERB BREAD

INGREDIENTS:

- 2 cups (225 g) almond flour
- 7 large eggs
- ⅓ cup (80 g) unsalted butter, melted
- ½ tsp. Xanthan Gum
- ¼ cup (20 g) Parmesan cheese, grated
- 2 Tbsp. olive oil
- 2 tsp. dried/fresh thyme

- 1 tsp. dried/fresh rosemary
- ½ tsp. garlic powder
- ½ tsp. onion powder
- ½ tsp. sea salt
- 1 tsp. keto baking powder

PROCESS:

1. Preheat the oven to 350°F (180°C) and line a 9x5-inch baking pan with parchment paper.

2. Beat the eggs until light and foamy. Add olive oil and melted butter and mix well.

3. Add flour, xanthan gum, Parmesan, and all the seasonings to the mixture and gently fold together with a spatula until thoroughly combined.

4. Pour this batter into the prepared tin and bake for 45 to 50 minutes or until a toothpick inserted into the center comes out clean.

5. Allow to cool for an hour before removing it from the pan. Transfer the loaf to a wire rack to cool completely.

6. Serve toasted with butter or melted cheese.

NUTRITION FACTS (Per Serving)

Calories: 232, Net Carbs: 2.6 g, Total Fat: 20.5 g, Cholesterol: 149 mg, Sodium: 158 mg,
Total Carbohydrate: 4.7 g, Fiber: 2.1 g, Total Sugars: 0.3 g, Protein: 8.4 g

CAULIFLOWER PIZZA BASE

INGREDIENTS:

- 2 cups (225 g) almond flour
- 1 cup (130 g) arrowroot flour
- 2 cups (200 g) cauliflower florets
- 1 whole egg
- 2 cloves of garlic

- 2 Tbsp. olive oil
- 1 tsp. sea salt

PROCESS:

1. Line a baking sheet with parchment paper and preheat the oven to 350°F (180°C).

2. Boil the cauliflower florets until soft, about 5 minutes, and drain. Transfer to a food processor and process until finely chopped.

3. Scrape down the sides of the food processor and add the egg and garlic. Process again until thoroughly combined.

4. Next, add almond flour, arrowroot flour, and salt. Process until everything is combined, taking care to scrape down the sides as necessary.

5. Transfer the mixture to the prepared baking sheet and spread it into the desired shape (I always go with an oval).

6. Drizzle the dough with olive oil and bake for 20 minutes until golden brown.

7. You can top this bread with tomatoes, mushrooms, Parmesan, and mozzarella.

NUTRITION FACTS (Per Serving)

Calories: 168, Net Carbs: 4.8 g, Total Fat: 13 g, Cholesterol: 20 mg, Sodium: 26 mg,
Total Carbohydrate: 7.7 g, Fiber: 2.9 g, Total Sugars: 0.7 g, Protein: 6 g

BAKING

Servings: 4 calzones

Prep Time: 15 minutes

Cook Time: 15 minutes

PEPPERONI CALZONE

INGREDIENTS:

- 1½ cups (170 g) almond flour
- 1¼ cups (140 g) shredded mozzarella
- 3 oz. (90 g) pepperoni, cubed
- ½ tsp. xanthan gum
- ¾ tsp. Italian seasoning
- ⅛ tsp. garlic powder
- ¼ cup (60 g) pizza sauce
- 3 Tbsp. water
- 1 Tbsp. olive oil

PROCESS:

1. Line a baking sheet with parchment paper and preheat the oven to 375°F (190°C).

2. Add Italian seasoning, flour, and garlic powder to a bowl, mix well, then add olive oil and water.

3. Knead with your hands until a smooth dough forms. Divide into four equal pieces and shape into balls.

4. Roll the balls out between two sheets of parchment paper until you have four circles roughly 6 inches in diameter each.

5. Spread pizza sauce onto the circles just like you would on a pizza base. Then, arrange the pepperoni and mozzarella cheese on half of each circle of dough.

6. Carefully fold the calzones in half and pinch the edges tightly over each other to form a seal.

7. Place the calzones in the oven for 15 minutes until lightly golden.

8. Serve hot.

NUTRITION FACTS (Per Serving)

Calories: 354, Net Carbs: 5.1 g, Total Fat: 29 g, Cholesterol: 30 mg, Sodium: 517 mg, Total Carbohydrate: 9.2 g, Fiber: 4.1 g, Total Sugars: 0.6 g, Protein: 14.2 g

FROM THE AUTHOR

My name is Jennifer Tate. I have been a **professional chef for over fifteen years** and am a passionate advocate for the **ketogenic diet.** I am highly recognized for making culinary magic in my home kitchen. I am also a busy mom of two. This means I am always on the run and looking for any chance to save time and money. With a passion for healthy living and first-hand knowledge of what it takes to stick to a successful lifestyle plan, I am prepared to be your guide throughout this journey.

This book teaches exactly the Mediterranean lifestyle and why so many people opt for this diet plan. We discuss the **healing benefits and key nutrition info** related to Mediterranean ketogenic eating.

However, consistency is key to following this diet—breakdowns can destroy the long work for your health. So I've developed simple recipes for the Mediterranean keto diet. **I eat them myself, feed them to my family, and include them in the meal plans for my clients.**

In addition to the recipes contained herein, I leave you a wide field for experiments. You can combine ingredients from the list of allowed keto products and create your masterpieces depending on your mood. But of course, don't forget the basics.

I generously share my Mediterranean keto recipes and mastery secrets with my readers. The ketogenic diet has never been so easy-to-follow and delicious. Let yourself enjoy your food every day!

OUR RECOMMENDATIONS

Keto Vegan Cookbook: Nutritious Plant-Based, Dairy-Free, Low-Carb Recipes for a Ketogenic Diet

Keto Bread Cookbook: Easy Keto Bread Recipes for Low-Carb Baking to Lose Weight Fast

Thank you, readers!

I am so grateful for those of you who make up the community of readers I love writing recipe books for! Thank you for your shares, encouraging emails, feedback, and reviews. I appreciate each one more than you guys knows!

If you have any questions, feel free to contact me

FACEBOOK

GOODREADS

Copyright

Printed in Great Britain
by Amazon